Supplement to

THE COMPLETE BOOK OF EMIGRANTS IN BONDAGE

1614-1775

Engraved for the Newgate Calendar.

Representation of the Transports going from Newgate to take water at Blackfriars.

Supplement to
THE
COMPLETE
BOOK OF
EMIGRANTS
IN
BONDAGE

1614 - 1775

Peter Wilson Coldham

GENEALOGICAL PUBLISHING CO., INC.

Copyright © 1992
Peter Wilson Coldham
Surrey, England
All Rights Reserved
Published by Genealogical Publishing Co., Inc.
1001 N. Calvert Street, Baltimore, MD 21202
Library of Congress Catalogue Card Number 92-81863
International Standard Book Number 978-0-8063-1345-0

Extracts from Crown Copyright Documents are published
by permission of Her Majesty's Stationery Office, and
grateful acknowledgement is made to the Bristol Record Office

Supplement to the Complete Book of Emigrants in Bondage 1614-1775

The publication in 1988 of *The Complete Book of Emigrants in Bondage 1614-1775*, which contained the names of some 45,000 English convicts sentenced to be transported to the American colonies, was based on a fifteen-year study of records compiled by the clerks of Assize and Quarter Sessions Courts. The very nature of the records themselves, their location and arrangement, make it inevitable that, as further archival resources become available, some additions and amendments become necessary.

An attempt has now been made to gather together material relating to transported convicts who either escaped detection altogether during the first round of researches or about whom newly accessible information has become available.

The principal archives examined or re-examined in order to compile the lists which follow have been:

Public Record Office

PATENT ROLLS, 1655-1719 (C66)

Because of the inadequate calendaring of this enormous series of parchment rolls, it was thought desirable to re-examine the collection. This has resulted in the identification of a few additional pardons on condition of transportation and the expansion of certain entries.

CRIMINAL CORRESPONDENCE, 1718-1775 (SP44)

The following volumes and papers in this class have been examined:

SP44/79–92. Appeals, Correspondence and Reprieves.

SP44/251–267. Entry Books of Petitions, 1718-1782.

This study has revealed that a good number of convicts who are recorded in the court records as having been sentenced to transportation were subsequently given a free pardon or had their sentence commuted on condition of serving in the Army or Navy.

STATE PAPERS (CRIMINAL)

These papers, which show a considerable overlap with Class C44, have also yielded a few additional details:

SP36/151–153 Law Officers' Reports, Petitions, etc., 1728–1760.

SP36/154–159. Petitions etc., undated temp. George II.

Bristol Record Office

As noted in the introduction (p. xiii) to Vol. 5 of *Bonded Passengers to America*[1], the City of Bristol by Royal Charter of 1373 was accorded the right to conduct its own Assize Courts. Correspondence with the Bristol Record Office in 1982, however, failed to reveal accessible sources which might be used to augment the data gleaned from central records. Further investigation has now identified documents relating to criminal transportation scattered amongst Bristol Quarter Sessions records, a series of Docket Books recording the names of those sentenced to transportation between 1722 and 1753, and a collection of bonds entered into with transportation contractors. With the help of the Bristol Record Office staff, the documents concerned have now been identified and transcriptions made from the following principal sources:

Sessions Docket Books, 1721–1753

Transportation Bonds, September 1759–May 1775

[1] Genealogical Publishing Co., Inc., 1983.

ABBREVIATIONS USED

•	=	Revision of original entry in *Complete Book of Emigrants in Bondage*
AT	=	Awaiting transportation
Bd	=	Bedfordshire
Be	=	Berkshire
Bu	=	Buckinghamshire
Ca	=	Cambridgeshire
Ch	=	Cheshire
Co	=	Cornwall
Cu	=	Cumberland
Db	=	Derbyshire
De	=	Devon
Do	=	Dorset
Du	=	Durham
E	=	Essex
Fl	=	Flint
G	=	Gloucestershire
Ha	=	Hampshire
He	=	Herefordshire
Ht	=	Hertfordshire
Hu	=	Huntingdonshire
K	=	Kent
La	=	Lancashire
LC	=	Landing Certificate
Le	=	Leicestershire
Li	=	Lincolnshire
M	=	Middlesex
Md	=	Maryland
Mo	=	Monmouthshire
NE	=	New England
Nf	=	Norfolk
Nl	=	Northumberland
No	=	Northamptonshire
Nt	=	Nottinghamshire

O	=	Oxfordshire
R	=	Reprieved for transportation
Ru	=	Rutlandshire
S	=	Sentenced to transportation
s	=	stealing
SC	=	South Carolina
Sh	=	Shropshire
SL	=	Sentenced at Southwark
So	=	Somerset
SP	=	State Papers
SQS	=	Sentenced at Quarter Sessions
St	=	Staffordshire
Su	=	Suffolk
SW	=	Sentenced at Westminster Sessions
SWK	=	Sentenced at West Kent Quarter Sessions
Sx	=	Sussex
Sy	=	Surrey
T	=	Transported
TB	=	Transportation Bond
Va	=	Virginia
Wa	=	Warwickshire
We	=	Westmorland
Wi	=	Wiltshire
Wo	=	Worcestershire
X	=	Stray records
Y	=	Yorkshire

Supplement to Emigrants in Bondage

• = Revised entry

- Abbott, Mary wife of John. S 14 yrs Apr but pardoned May 1773. M.
- Abraham, John of Lambeth. SQS Jan 1769 & TB *Thornton* but pardoned in same month. Sy.
- Abraham, Judith wife of Solomon, R Oct 1771 & TB by *Justitia* but taken from ship & pardoned Nov 1771. M.
- Abraham, Thomas. S Summer 1746 R 14 yrs Apr 1747. De.
- Abrahams, John. S Lent 1773 [*not 1733*]. Bd.
- Acton, John. R & T for life Apr 1769 *Tryal*. K.
  Adams, John. S Summer 1741 R 14 yrs Feb 1742. Ha.
  Adams, Jonathan. S 14 yrs Bristol for receiving Aug 1759 TB to Md Apr 1760. G.
- Adams, Robert. S s mare Summer 1765 R 14 yrs Lent 1765. Li.
- Adams, Sarah. S Mar R Jun 1758 T 14 yrs Apr 1759 *Thetis*. Ht.
  Addison, James of St. Martin in Fields. R Jun 1714 & to remain in Newgate until transported. M.
  Adey, Benjamin. S Bristol Feb 1727. G.
  Adey, John. S Bristol Sep 1726. G.
- Adlington, George. S Lent T Apr 1758 *Lux* from London. Db.
  Alder, Ann (1765). *See* Stanley. M.
  Aldin, Charles. S Bristol Mar AT Apr 1745. G.
- Alett, John of Rotherhithe. SQS Jan 1762 & TB *Neptune* but R for Army service in Jamaica Apr 1762. Sy.
  Alford, James. SQS Bristol Mar TB to Md Apr 1769. G.
- Allard, William. S s chain at Upton upon Severn Lent R for Army service Jly 1761; found at large in Severnstoke & R 14 yrs Summer 1765. Wo.
  Allen, George. S Lent R 14 yrs Jun 1746. De.
- Allen, George. SQS May TB Jly 1773 *Tayloe*, removed from ship on appeal but unsuccessful & law to take its course. M.
- Allen, James. S & TB Apr 1762 *Dolphin* but R to serve in Army in Jamaica Apr 1762. L.
- Allen, John. SQS May TB Jly 1773 *Tayloe*, removed from ship on appeal but unsuccessful & law to take its course. M.
- Allen, Mary wife of Matterdell. S May 1766 & TB *Justitia*, but pardoned Aug 1766. M.
- Allen, Thomas. S Summer 1760 but R for Army service Aug 1761. G.

Allen, William. R Nov 1769. Do.
Alnutt, Margaret. SQS Bristol Mar TB to Md May 1763. G.
Anderson *alias* Anson, Andrew. R 14 yrs Bristol Sep 1749. G.
Anderson, Hester, singlewoman. S Bristol Apr 1743. G.
Anderson, James. SQS Bristol Dec 1773 TB to Va May 1774.
Anderson, Peter. S Bristol Apr 1745. G.
Anderson, Richard. S Summer 1727 R Jly 1728. Li.
• Andrews, Jasper. S Mar 1720 R & T Jan 1722 *Gilbert* LC Annapolis Jly 1722. L.
• Andrews, John. R 14 yrs May 1735. Wi.
Andrews, John. R for life for forgery May 1750. L.
• Andrews, William TB Apr 1762 *Neptune* but R for Army service in Jamaica same month. K.
Angemenny, Isaac. S Bristol Aug 1729. G.
• Angus, Robert. S Oct 1771 TB *Justitia*, taken from ship & pardoned Nov 1771. L.
• Ansell, John. SQS May 1764 but pardoned Sep 1764. Ha.
Anson, Andrew (1749). *See* Anderson. G.
Applebee, Thomas. S Bristol Mar 1737. G.
Archer, Judith (1750). *See* Butler. M.
• Archer, William. S Jan-Feb 1774 but pardoned Mar 1774. M.
Arkill, Edward. SQS Bristol Aug TB to Va Sep 1773. G.
• Armer, John. R Jly 1775 to be T 14 yrs but taken from ship & pardoned same month. M.
• Armstrong, John. R 14 yrs Apr T Dec 1771 *Justitia*. K.
• Armstrong *alias* Welchman, Samuel. R Jan T Jly 1722 *Alexander* to Nevis or Jamaica. M.
Arnold, Hannah. R 14 yrs Bristol Sep 1742. G.
Arnold, John. SQS Bristol Jan TB to Md Apr 1768. G.
• Arnold, Rowland. S Sep sentence confirmed & T Dec 1767 *Neptune*. L.
• Arthur, Hannah. R Feb for firing barn T 14 yrs Nov 1762 *Prince William*. K.
Arthur, Mary wife of William. SQS Bristol Jun 1771 TB to Va Feb 1772. G.
Arthurs, Ann of Bristol, widow. SQS Bristol Oct TB Nov 1755. G.
Ash, Edward of Stogumber, cheeseman. R for Barbados Feb 1683. So.
Ash, John. S Mar R Jly 1728. Do.
Ash, Thomas. S Lent R Jly 1726. Do.
Ashford, Ann, widow. SQS Bristol Mar TB to Va Apr 1773. G.
• Ashman, Isaac. S Lent R Jun 1734. So.
Ashmore, William. S Bristol Apr 1743. G.
• Ashton, Joseph. T *Expedition* from Bristol to South Carolina 1728. G.
Ashworth, John. S Bristol Dec 1748. G.
Aspinall, Richard. Ordered to be taken from *Tryal* Jly 1753.
• Aspiner, John. SWK Jly 1772 & respited same month. K.

Asplin, Minah (1775). *See* Rutter. Sh.
• Atherton, Robert. S Lent R Jly T Sep 1730 *Smith*. Sy.
Atkins, John. S Bristol Feb 1751. G.
Atkinson, Elizabeth, spinster. SQS Hull Jly TB Aug 1766. Y.
• Atkinson, John. R Jun T 14 yrs Dec 1758 *The Brothers*. K.
Atkinson, John. S Lent R Jly 1764. K.
• Atkinson, John of St. Martin in Fields. SW Apr 1773 but pardoned same month. M.
Attwell, Lucretia Diana Arabella. S Bristol Sep 1735. G.
Austin, John. R 14 yrs Bristol Oct 1740. G.
• Aylsbury, Thomas. S Jly TB Sep 1767 *Justitia* but taken from ship & pardoned same month. M.
Ayres, John of Hartley Wintney. R for America Jly 1696. Ha.
Ayers, Mary wife of Samuel. SQS Hull Easter 1760 TB Jan 1761. Y.

Baber, Stephen. S Bristol Sep 1754. G.
Babos, Patrick. SQS Bristol Dec 1760 TB to Md Apr 1761. G.
Backway, Margery. R 14 yrs Jun 1768. Co.
Badham, Edward. R 14 yrs Apr 1771. He.
• Bagley, Edward of Rotherhithe, broker. SQS Jan 1765 TB *Ann* but pardoned Feb 1765. Sy.
Baigeant, Robert. R 14 yrs Feb 1764. Ha.
• Bailey, Elizabeth. S Lent but pardoned Apr 1770. Le.
• Bailey, Frances [*not Francis*]. S Jan-Feb 1775 but taken from ship & pardoned Apr 1775. M.
Bailey, Matthew of Leeds. R for Africa or America Jly 1715. Y.
Baker, Elizabeth. R 14 yrs Apr 1771. Sh.
• Baker, Isaac. S Lent R 14 yrs Jly 1725. Wi.
Baker, James. S Bristol Sep 1734. G.
Baker, Samuel. Baker, Samuel. S Summer 1764 R 14 yrs Jan 1765. K.
• Baker, Susannah. S & TB Sep 1764 *Justitia* but pardoned Nov 1764. M.
• Baker, Thomas. R 14 yrs Mar 1761 TB to Va but R for Army service Jly 1761. De.
• Baker, Thomas. S Dec 1761 TB *Dolphin* but R for Army service same month. M.
Baker, Thomas. R to T himself for 7 yrs for grand larceny May 1764. L.
Ball, John. SQS Bristol Feb TB to Md May 1763. G.
Ball, William. S Summer 1743 R 14 yrs Feb 1744. Co.
• Balm, John. R Jun R Jan T 14 yrs Sep 1765 *Justitia*. Ht.
• Banford, James. S Lent R 14 yrs Jun 1744. Ha.
Banks, Catherine. S (Bristol) Feb 1722. G.
Bannister, Elizabeth, singlewoman. S Bristol Jan 1741. G.
Bannister, John. SQS Bristol Jun TB to Md Aug 1769. G.

Banister, Thomas. SQS Bristol May TB to Va Aug 1774. G.
Barber, Jane, spinster. S Bristol Sep 1737. G.
Barber, Samuel (1761). *See* Gill. Le.
* Barew, Abraham. S May T Jly 1771 *Scarsdale*; unexpired time remitted Aug 1775. M.
Barker, John. S Lent R Jun 1723. Bd.
Barker, John of St. Nicholas. S Bristol Sep 1752. G.
* Barker, Joseph. S Jly 1773 but taken from ship & pardoned same month. L.
* Barker, Samuel. TB 14 yrs Sep 1765 *Justitia* but pardoned same month. K.
* Barlow, Samuel. S Dec 1764 TB Jan 1765 *Tryal* but pardoned Apr 1765. M.
* Barnard, Edward. S Summer 1724 R Jan T 14 yrs Sep 1765 *Justitia*. E.
* Barnes, William. R for sacrilege May T 14 yrs Nov 1762 *Prince William*. L.
Barnet, Daniel. S Summer 1730 s horse R Feb 1731. Co.
* Barrett, Edward. SQS Feb TB *Thornton* but pardoned for sea service Mar 1772. M.
* Barrett, Nathaniel. S Lent R 14 yrs Summer 1760. Sy.
Barrett, William (1731). *See* Taylor. Wi.
Barrow, Mary, spinster. S Bristol May 1736. G.
Barrow, Patience (1746). *See* Berrow. G.
Barrs, Richard. SQS Bristol Dec 1765 TB to Md Apr 1766. G.
Barry, George. S Bristol Nov 1737. G.
Bartlett, Cornelius of Ugborough, husbandman. R for America Jly 1696. De.
Bartlet, Mary, widow. S Bristol Sep 1730. G.
* Barto, Samuel. S Summer 1746 for murder of a bastard child R for life Feb 1747. De.
Barton, Thomas. R for cutting hop binds in a plantation Jan 1737. Ha.
Basely, Thomas (1724). *See* Saunders. Co.
Bass, William (1761). *See* Gill. Le.
Bassett, Robert. S Bristol Apr 1745. G.
Basset, William. R for life Feb 1767. G.
* Batt, George. S Lent R 14 yrs May 1731. Do.
Battersby, Thomas. R Jun 1714 & to remain in Newgate until transported. L.
* Baughurst, Richard. S s at Shinfield Lent 1769, case reviewed but law to take its course. Be.
* Baumer, William. R Jun T 14 yrs Dec 1758 *The Brothers*. K.
Bavington, Ann. S Summer 1773. Bu.
* Bawden, Henry. R 14 yrs Aug 1738, found at large & R 14 yrs Jan 1746. Co.

- Baxter *alias* Jones, Mary, *alias* Black Moll. S Summer 1752 R 14 yrs Feb 1753; found at large May & T for life Sep 1758 *Tryal*. De.

  Baxter, Samuel of Riccall. SQS Beverley Michaelmas 1741. Y.

  Bayliss, James. R for life for highway robbery in Ledbury, Herefordshire, Jly 1736. LM.
- Baylis, William. S Lent R 14 yrs Jun 1744. So.

  Bayliss, William. R 14 yrs May 1768. Wo.

  Bazer *alias* Lewis, John. S Jly 1757 R 14 yrs Feb 1758. Wi.
- Bean, Daniel. S Jan-Feb taken from ship & pardoned Apr 1774. M.
- Bean *alias* Macoppy, Jane. R Jan T 14 yrs Jly 1722 *Alexander* to Nevis or Jamaica. M.

  Bear, Timothy. S Summer 1743 R 14 yrs Feb 1744. Co.
- Beard, John. SQS Oct 1761 TB *Dolphin* but R for Army service same month. M.

  Beauchamp, John. S Summer 1743 R Feb T May 1744 *Justitia*. Sy.

  Beaumont, Samuel. S Lent R Jun 1724. Li.
- Beaver, Ann. S Apr-May T Jly 1771 *Scarsdale* but taken from ship & pardoned same month. M.

  Bee, George. SQS Hull Epiphany 1754. Y.
- Beeby, George of Bilston. R for parts overseas Jly 1719. St.
- Beeby, Richard of Bilston. R for parts overseas Jly 1719. St.
- Beer, Hugh, *alias* Thomas, William. R 14 yrs Jan 1736. So.
- Beer, Josias. R 14 yrs May 1735. De.

  Beir, Mary, spinster. S Bristol Mar 1741. G.
- Bell, Hannah. S Oct but taken from ship & pardoned Nov 1774. L.

  Bell, William (1746). *See* Forster, Robert. Nl.
- Bellchamber, Elizabeth. S Mar R Jun T 14 yrs Dec 1758 *The Brothers*. Sx.

  Bemen, Thomas. S Lent R Jly 1724. Wi.
- Bendall, Christopher. S Mar TB Oct 1735; found at large & R Jun 1736. Wi.

  Bendall, William. S Bristol Feb AT Apr 1745. G.
- Benham, John. R Jun as agreeing to amputation of limb to test styptic R & T for life Sep 1767 *Justitia*. M.
- Benison, Joseph. S Lent R 14 yrs May 1731. So.
- Bennett, Edward. R & T for life Apr 1770 *New Trial*. Sy.

  Bennett, John (1761). *See* Cade. L.

  Bennett, John (1768). *See* Benny. M.

  Bennett, Nicholas of St. James Westminster. R for Barbados or Jamaica Aug 1700. M.

  Bennet, Thomas. S Bristol Feb 1741. G.
- Benny *alias* Bennett, John. SQS s dog collars May, case reviewed unfavourably T Oct 1768 *Justitia*. M.

  Benson, Mary. S Bristol May 1731. G.

  Benwick, William. R for life Apr 1774. Sy.

Berk, Thomas (1772). *See* Hollis. M.
Berkley, William (1769). *See* Forsith, John. Sy.
Berrett, Isaac. SQS Bristol Sep 1763 TB to Md Apr 1764. G.
Berrow *alias* Barrow, Patience, singlewoman. S Bristol Apr 1746. G.
Berry, George of Bilston. R for T overseas Jly 1719. St.
Berry, James. SQS Summer 1768. Ha.
Berry, Richard of Lincoln[shire]. R for America Feb 1696. Li.
- Bess, Edward. S Bristol Apr 1767 R 14 yrs & TB to Md Sep 1768. G.
Best, Thomas of York. R for America or Africa Mar 1719. Y.
Bettalake, Elizabeth. S for murdering her bastard child Lent R Jly 1724. De
Bettlestone, Margaret. SQS for s provisions Jan 1770. Sh.
Bettlestone, William. SQS 14 yrs for receiving stolen goods Jan 1770. Sh.
Bevan, Mary. S Bristol Mar 1738. G.
- Bevan, Thomas. S Bristol Apr 1767 R 14 yrs & TB to Md Sep 1768. G.
Bever, John (1767). *See* Vevers. L.
Bickham, Thomas. S Bristol Oct 1744. G.
Bicknell, Susannah. SQS Dec 1763 TB to Md Apr 1764. G.
Biddlecombe, John. S Summer 1741 R 14 yrs Feb 1742. Ha.
Bidds, Riley. S Bristol Dec 1734. G.
Biddulph, John. SQS Lent 1775. St.
- Biggs, Richard. R 14 yrs Jun 1760 TB to Va Mar 1761 but R for Army service abroad Apr 1761. Wi.
- Biggs, Stephen. S for highway robbery at Hardwick & R Summer 1773. Bu.
Bigwood, James. SQS Bristol Mar TB to Va May 1775. G.
- Billing, William. S Summer 1727 R Jly TB to Md Aug 1728. Db.
Billingsley, William of Beckbury. R for Barbados Jly 1663. Sh.
- Bilton, Robert. S & R for life s horse Aug 1767, shipwrecked on passage Nov 1770 & pardoned Apr 1771. Nl.
Binny, John. S Bristol Jun 1734. G.
- Birch, Ann, soldier's wife. S & T Apr 1769 *Tryal* but taken from ship & pardoned same month. L.
- Birch, William. R Aug 1774 but taken from ship & pardoned same month. Y.
Bird, Charles, a boy. S Lent R Jly 1728. Wa.
- Bird, John. SQS Jly T Oct 1768 *Justitia* but taken from ship & pardoned same month. M.
Birde, John. S Jly but pardoned Aug 1773. L.
Bird, Judith. SQS Hull Sep 1748. Y.
- Bird, Thomas. S for setting fire to corn stack & R Summer 1772 but pardoned Oct 1772. Wa.
Birt, Teressa, spinster. SQS Bristol Nov 1771 TB to Va Feb 1772. G.

Bishop, Daniel. R for life for murder Bristol Apr 1752. G.
Bishop, Elizabeth. SQS Bristol & TB to Md Sep 1761. G.
- Bishop, George. S May 1721 R Jan T 14 yrs Jly 1722 *Alexander*. L.
- Bishop, John. S Summer 1740 R 14 yrs Apr 1741. So.
Bishop, Mary, singlewoman. S Bristol Jan 1739. G.
- Bishop, Mary. S Lent for arson R 14 yrs Jun 1744 TB to Va 1745. De.
Bishop, Solomon, weaver. S Bristol Sep 1742. G.
Bishop, William of Derby[shire]. R for America Feb 1696. Db.
- Bishop, William. S Summer 1741 R Feb T Apr 1742 *Bond*. E.
- Blackburne, John. R Jun T 14 yrs Sep 1766 *Justitia*. E.
- Blackburn, Matthew. S for highway robbery Lent R Jun TB to Md Aug 1727. Db.
Blackford, Thomas *alias* William. R 14 yrs Jun 1765. Sx.
Blackford, William (1765). *See* Blackford, Thomas.
Black Moll (1752). *See* Baxter, Mary. De.
Blackmore, William. S Summer 1742 R 14 yrs Feb 1743. So.
- Blackwell, Deborah. S Sep-Oct TB Dec *Justitia* but pardoned Nov 1771. M.
Blackwood, John. S Gt. Yarmouth Sep 1763 R 14 yrs Oct 1764. Nf.
- Blake, John. S s at Thwaite & R Lent but pardoned Apr 1773. Su.
- Bland, Arthur. S Lent but taken from ship & pardoned Apr 1771. No.
Bland, John. SQS Bristol Aug TB to Va Sep 1773. G.
- Bland, Thomas. SQS Oct TB *Justitia* but taken from ship & pardoned for sea service Nov 1771. M.
- Blewitt, William. R Jun 1723 T 14 yrs Dec 1724 *Rappahannock* to Va. M.
Blite, Mary, spinster. S Bristol Apr 1745. G.
- Blight, Robert [*not Roger*]. S Summer 1741 R 14 yrs Feb 1742. De.
- Blundell, John. S Lent & R 14 yrs but R to serve in 49th Regiment in Jamaica Apr 1761. Sy.
- Boatman, George. R Feb T 14 yrs May 1736 *Patapsco*. E.
Boland, Jane. S Bristol Mar 1741. G.
Bolton, John of Preshute, blacksmith. R for Barbados Jly 1671. Wi.
Bond, Brian. S Lent R Jly 1726. So.
- Bond, Edward. T *Expedition* from Bristol to South Carolina 1728. Wi.
- Boney, Judith [*not Julia*] of St. Margaret, Westminster, spinster. SW Apr 1774 but taken from ship & pardoned. M.
- Booth, Ann. S Jan-Feb TB *Thornton* but pardoned Mar 1771. M.
Boothe, William. R 14 yrs Feb 1765. Ch.
Bore *alias* Fewtrell, Charles. S Summer 1723 R Feb 1724. Sh.
Borough, George. S 14 yrs Bristol & TB to Md Apr 1764. G.
- Bossom, Charles. S s at St. Giles, Reading, Lent but pardoned Apr 1748. Be.
Bostock *alias* Head, Mary. R Jan 1722. LM.
- Bostock, William. S for burglary Summer R 14 yrs Aug 1763. Sh.

15

- Boswell, Henry. S City Mar for sacrilege R 14 yrs May 1752. Y.
- Boswell, John. S Bristol May 1763 R 14 yrs & TB to Md Apr 1764. G.

Bosworth, George of Derby[shire]. R for America Feb 1696. Db.
- Bothams, John. S Summer 1726 R Jun TB to Md Aug 1727. Db.
- Bouchier [*not Southier*], James, gent. R for America Nov 1706. L.
- Bould, John. S s horse & R for life Apr 1766. St.

Boulton, Ann, spinster. SQS Bristol Mar TB to Va May 1775. G.

Bourne, Ann. SQS Bristol Aug TB to Md Sep 1759. G.

Bourne, Thomas of Norwich. R Jly 1703. Nf.

Bowcher, Francis of Lyme Regis, husbandman. R for Barbados Feb 1671. Do.

Bowdey, Richard of Egham. R for Barbados Jun 1671. Sy.

Bowerman, Edward. S Bristol Mar TB to Md Apr 1765. G.
- Bowers, Thomas, *alias* Horton, John. S Lent R 14 yrs Summer but R for Army service Jly 1760. Wo.
- Bowler, John. S Oct TB *Justitia* but taken from ship & pardoned Nov 1771. L.

Bowles, George. R 14 yrs Jun 1768. So.

Bowles, William. SQS Summer 1767. Wi.

Bowman, George. S Bristol Aug 1753. G.

Bowman, John. SQS Hull & TB Oct 1765. Y.

Bowman, Thomas. S Bristol Aug AT Sep 1742. G.

Bowyer, Mary. R 14 yrs Jun 1758. Ha.
- Bowyer, Thomas. S & T Jly *Tayloe* but taken from ship & pardoned Jly 1772. M.

Brabant, John. S Lent R 14 yrs Jun 1753. Co.
- Brackleyhurst or Brocklehurst, William. S May TB *Prince William* but pardoned Jly 1762. M.
- Bradbury, John. S s mare & R Lent but pardoned May 1763. Bu.

Bradford, John. SQS Bristol Jly AT Aug 1775. G.
- Bradley, Edward. S for coining Lent R Jly T Sep 1730 *Smith*. Ht.
- Bradley, Thomas. S Lent R Jun 1724, died on *Rappahannock* on passage to America 1726. Li.

Bradley, William. SQS Hull & TB Jan 1761. Y.
- Bradrilk, James [*not Christopher*]. S Lent R Jly T Dec 1731 *Forward*. Sy.
- Brathwaite, Matthew. S Jly 1760 & R for sea service Feb 1761. Ha.
- Brambleby, William Henry. R May T 14 yrs Sep 1767 *Justitia*. K.
- Brandon, William. SQS Summer but pardoned Oct 1774. Ht.
- Brazier, Richard. S s sheep Summer R for life Aug 1769. He.
- Bray, John. S Lent R Jun T 14 yrs Oct 1738 *Genoa*. Sy.

Brayley, Ann. SQS Bristol Aug TB to Md Sep 1766 LC Annapolis from *Randolph* Mar 1767. G.
- Breakspear, Jane wife of John. S Apr but pardoned May 1773. M.

Breare, David. R 7yrs Feb 1767. Ha.

- Brentnall, William. S s heifers Lent R 14 yrs Summer 1760; found at large but pardoned Aug 1764. Nf.
Brewer, John, blacksmith. R (Bristol) for America Jly 1696. G.
Brewer, William. S Bristol Jun AT Sep 1740. G.
- Brice, Robert. S Summer 1740 R 14 yrs Feb 1741. Ha.
Bridges, Elizabeth. S Lent R 14 yrs Jly 1742. Sy.
Bridgman, Francis Swanston. SQS Bristol Dec 1774 TB to Va May 1775. G.
Bright, John (1749). *See* Bryant. G.
- Bright, Thomas. S Jan-Feb but taken from ship & pardoned Apr 1774. M.
Bright, William of Pimm(?). R for America Jly 1696. De.
Brigman, Thomas of Warbleton, husbandman. R for Barbados Jun 1671. Sx.
Brikham, George. S Bristol Jun 1726. G.
Brint, Ezekiel. S Bristol Apr 1741. G.
Brisk *alias* Brisko, Robert of Burstwick. SQS Beverley Michaelmas 1740. Y.
Britt, John of Redriffe. R for Barbados Jun 1671. Sy.
- Brittain, James. S Aug 1757 R Feb T 14 yrs Sep 1758 *Tryal.* K.
Britten, William (1769). *See* Diddle. G.
- Britton, Samuel. TB Apr 1765 *Ann* but pardoned same month. M.
- Broadwood, James. S Jan TB *Thornton* but pardoned Jan 1772. M.
- Bromidge, James. S Summer T Sep 1770 but taken from ship at Bristol & pardoned. Wa.
- Brook, William. S Summer 1741 R 14 yrs Feb 1742. So.
- Brookland, John. S s at Cookham Lent but pardoned Apr 1769. Be.
Brooks, Ann. R 14 yrs Bristol Oct 1754 & Aug 1755. G.
Brookes, John of Braintree. R for Barbados Jun 1671. E.
Brooks, John. S Bristol Nov 1739. G.
- Broom, John. R Jan T Jly 1722 *Alexander* to Nevis or Jamaica. M.
Broome, John. SQS Bristol Jly 1772 AT Apr 1773. G.
Broughton, Mary. SQS Summer 1768. Sh.
Broughton, William. S Bristol Mar 1747. G.
Broughton, William (1752). *See* Sparrow. So.
- Brown, Bartholomew. S Sep TB *Justitia* but pardoned for sea service Dec 1771. M.
Brown, Betty Jr. R 14 yrs Apr 1771. G.
- Brown, Charles. S s at Belford Summer 1769 T *Caesar* & shipwrecked on passage; R for sea service Dec 1770. Nl.
Brown, Elizabeth. S Jly 1750. Taken from *Eagle* on appeal of inhabitants of Drayton, Salop, but ordered to be T 8 Nov 1751. Li.
Brown, George. SQS Bristol Jly 1772 TB to Va Apr 1773. G.
- Brown, Hugh. R for life Sep 1764 TB to Va 1765. De.
- Brown, James. R 14 yrs May 1735. Ha.

- Brown, James. S s silver tumbler at St. Mary, Stafford, Lent 1761 T *Atlas* from Bristol, pardoned for being at large Jun 1763. St.
  Brown, James. R for highway robbery Feb 1764. K.
- Brown, James. R & T 14 yrs Apr 1769 *Forward*. K.
  Browne, John of Exeter, alehouse keeper. R for America Jly 1696. De.
  Brown, John. S Summer 1726 R Jun 1727. Wa.
  Brown, John. SQS Bristol Aug 1760 TB to Md Apr 1761. G.
  Brown, John. S for highway robbery Summer 1772 R 14 yrs Lent 1773. Nf.
- Brown, Joseph. R & T 14 yrs Apr 1769 *Tryal*. K.
- Brown, Mark. S Jan-Feb but taken from ship & pardoned Apr 1774. M.
- Brown, Mary wife of Daniel. S Jan R 14 yrs Jun 1746 TB to Va Jun 1747.
- Brown, Mary. S Apr respited May 1775. M.
- Brown, Richard. S Apr pardoned May 1773. L.
  Brown, Thomas. S Summer 1727 R Jly 1728. Li.
- Brown, Thomas. S Lent R 14 yrs Summer 1760 pardoned for Army service Jly 1761. St.
  Brown, William. S Summer 1727 R Jly 1728. Wa.
- Browning, George the younger. S Bristol Apr 1773 R for life & TB to Va May 1774.
- Browning, John. S Summer 1743 R Feb T May 1744 *Justitia*. Sx.
  Browning, John. SQS Bristol Feb TB to Va May 1774. G.
  Browning, Thomas. S Lent R 14 yrs Jun 1738. K.
  Bryant *alias* Bright, John. S Bristol Jun AT Aug 1749. G.
- Bryant, Thomas. R Feb T 14 yrs Jun 1764 *Dolphin*. K.
  Bryant, Thomas. SQS Bristol Oct 1764 TB to Md Apr 1765. G.
- Buchanon, Alexander. SWK Apr but pardoned on appeal of father Alexander B. May 1772. K.
  Buck, Edward. S Bristol Sep 1734. G.
  Buck, Robert. SQS Hull Easter 1749. Y.
  Bucknall, Humphrey of Birmingham. R for America Feb 1680. Wa.
- Budd, Thomas. S Lent R 14 yrs Jly 1724. De.
  Budden, Elias. R 14 yrs Sep 1768. Ha.
  Buffield, Isaac. R for Barbados or Jamaica Mar 1688. L.
- Bulger, Mary. S Sep 1758 R Oct 1761 T for life Apr 1762 *Dolphin*. L.
- Bull, Jane. TB *Tryal* but pardoned Dec 1765. M.
- Bulling, Richard. R Jun 1737 T Jan 1738 *Dorsetshire*. E.
- Bullock, James. S Lent R Jun T 14 yrs Oct 1738 *Genoa*. Sx.
- Bullock, William. S & R Lent 1769, case reviewed unfavourably. St.
  Bulmerink, John. S Bristol Dec 1747. G.
- Bulney, John. S Summer 1734 R Feb T 14 yrs Apr 1735 *Patapsco*. Sy.
  Burchell, Charles. R Feb 1721. De.
  Burden, William of Newport Pagnell. R for Barbados Jan 1665. Bu.

- Burdett, John. S Jly 1761 but pardoned same month to enlist in 49th Regiment in Jamaica. L.

Burgis, James of Wotton under Edge. R for parts overseas Jly 1719. G.

Burges, John (1773). *See* Evans. St.

- Burges, Thomas. S Sep-Oct TB *Justitia* but pardoned Oct 1771. M.

Burk, Mary wife of Patrick. S Bristol Aug 1749. G.

- Burn, Ann. S s cloth Lent 1770 T *Caesar* but shipwrecked on passage & pardoned Dec 1770. Nl.
- Burret [*not Barritt*], Thomas. S Lent R Jun 1724 but died on passage in *Rappahannock* 1726. Li.
- Burridge, Robert. S for life for highway robbery Nov 1750. M.
- Burrows, Charles. S Lent R Jly T 14 yrs Sep 1742 *Forward*. Sy.

Burroughs, Frances wife of William. S Bristol Aug TB to Md Sep 1759. G.

- Burton, William. S Lent T Apr 1758 *Lux* from London. Db.
- Busby, Joseph. S Lent R Jun T Jly 1723 *Alexander* but died on passage. Bu.
- Butcher, James. S Lent R Jun T Oct 1724 *Forward* LC Annapolis Md Jun 1725. Sy.

Butcher, William. R 14 yrs Sep 1774. Sx.

Butler, John. R 14 yrs Jun 1768. Co.

Butler, John. S Bristol Feb 1739. G.

- Butler *alias* Archer *alias* Ogden, Judith. R 14 yrs Jly 1750. M.
- Butler, Richard. S Summer 1741 R Feb T 14 yrs Apr 1742 *Bond*. Bu.

Buttrey, Thomas. SQ Lent 1770. Sh.

- Cade *alias* Bennett, John. S Oct 1761 but R for Army service same month. L.

Caear, Thomas (1767). *See* Kear. G.

Callahan, Peter. SQS Bristol Aug 1764 TB to Md Apr 1765. G.

Camb, John. R Feb 1730. E.

- Cambridge, Martha, spinster. S Bristol Apr R 7 yrs & TB to Va Jly 1772. G.

Cambridge, Nathaniel. R for life Feb 1767. G.

- Campion, Robert. S Feb 1761 but R for sea service same month. L.

Candy, Elizabeth, spinster. SQS Bristol Feb TB to Va Mar 1771. G.

Canniver, Robert. SQS Bristol Aug 1764 TB to Md Apr 1765. G.

Canter, John. S Summer 1739 R 14 yrs Feb 1740. Co.

- Card, Peter. R for revealing names of accomplices & T for life May 1767 *Thornton*. Sx.

Cardiff, Christopher. R 14 yrs Jun 1768. So.

- Care, William. S Summer 1729 R 14 yrs Feb 1731. Wi.
- Carey, George. SWK Oct TB *Justitia* but taken from ship & pardoned for sea service Oct 1771. K.

- Cary, William. S Jly TB *Prince William* but R to serve in Army in Jamaica Jly 1762. M.

Carle, Charles. S (Bury St. Edmunds) s gelding Lent R 14 yrs Summer 1767. Su.

Carnaby, Edward. S Lent R Jun 1724. Li.

Carpenter, Edward, sawyer. S Bristol Jan 1737. G.
- Carpenter, Martha. S Feb but taken from ship & pardoned Apr 1775. L.

Carpenter, Thomas. S Lent R Jun 1730. Sy.
- Carrington, Daniel. S & R to T himself Oct 1761. L.

Carrill, Ann, wife of Thomas, tailor. R 14 yrs Bristol Sep 1745. G.

Carroll, John (1773). *See* Davis. G.

Carter, Bridget wife of John. SQS Bristol Mar TB to Va May 1775. G.

Carter, Charles of Bishops Hatfield. R for Barbados or Jamaica Mar 1709. Ht.
- Carter, Francis. S Bristol Apr R 14 yrs & TB to Va Jly 1772. G.

Carter *alias* Halsey, John. R Jun 1714 & to remain in Newgate until transported. L.
- Carter, John. S for highway robbery R Apr T Oct 1730 *Forward* but died on passage. M.
- Carter, John of Houghton. S s sheep in Tillbrook Summer 1767 R 14 yrs Lent 1768 but pardoned on petition of Mayor of Bedford. Bd.
- Carter, Robert. R Apr T 14 yrs Dec 1771 *Justitia*. Sy.

Carter, Sarah. S Bristol Apr 1743. G.

Carter, Thomas. S Summer 1767 R 14 yrs Lent 1768. Bd.
- Carter, William. TB *Forward* but pardoned on petition of inhabitants of Hoddesdon Apr 1723. Ht.

Carter, William. R for life Feb 1767. G.

Carwell, Nicholas. S Bristol Aug 1724. G.
- Carwithen, Susannah. S for murder of her bastard child Summer 1746 R for life Feb 1747. De.
- Castle, John. S Sep 1771 TB *Justitia* but respited on appeal of parents. M.

Caton, Samuel. S Lent R 14 yrs Jun 1738. Sy.
- Cavenaugh, Thomas. S Jan-Feb TB Apr 1772 *Thornton* but to T himself Sep 1772; pardoned Jan 1773. M.

Cavener, Daniel, tailor. S Bristol Jan 1734. G.

Chaddock, John, yeoman. S Bristol Dec 1733. G.

Challenger, Mary. S Lent R 14 yrs Jun 1744. So.

Chambers, William (1747). *See* Giles, Thomas. E.
- Chambers, William. S s sheep at Bradwell Abbey & R 14 yrs Lent 1774 [*not 1744*]. Bu.
- Chamneys, John. S Lent R Jun T 14 yrs Oct 1738 *Genoa*. Sx.
- Chandler, Joseph. SQS Oct but pardoned Nov 1772. M.

Chanter, John. R Jun 1736. De.

Chaplin *alias* Chapman, Richard of Enfield. R for Barbados Sep 1677. M.
Chapman, John. S Summer 1739 R Feb 1740. K.
• Chapman, Joseph. S May R Jun 1723 T 14 yrs *Alexander* LC Md Sep 1723. M.
• Chapman, Nathaniel. S Apr-May but taken from ship & pardoned Jly 1775. M.
Chapman, Richard (1677). *See* Chaplin. M.
• Chapman, William. S 14 yrs for receiving Summer but R to serve in Army in Jamaica Oct 1762. No.
• Chapple *alias* Sampson, Ambrose. S Mar 1730 R 14 yrs May 1731. So.
Charles, Thomas (1719). *See* James. Mo.
Charlesworth, Michael. S Summer 1727 R Jly 1728. Wa.
• Charriton [*not Cherriton*], John. S Bristol Apr R 7 yrs & TB to Va Jly 1772. G.
Cheek, John. R for life Feb 1767. Be.
• Cheeseman, William. S Summer 1737 R Feb T 14 yrs Jun 1738 *Forward*. Sx.
• Cherry, Elias. S May-Jly but taken from ship & pardoned Dec 1772. M.
Chester, Samuel SQS Lent 1774. Sh.
• Chilson, Brown. R Feb T 14 yrs Jun 1764 *Dolphin*. E.
• Chilton, Alice of St. Mary Savoy, spinster. R for Barbados Sep 1677. M.
Chilvers, Susan (1704). *See* Lewis. M.
Chin, Francis. S Lent R Jly 1724. So.
• Chipper, Edward. S Summer but pardoned Sep 1775. Sy.
 • Chipperfield, James. S Jly 1758 R Feb T 14 yrs Apr 1759 *Thetis*. E.
Chirnside, Margaret, aged 22, servant. SQS Easter 1775 but given free pardon in 1777. Nl.
• Chitty, George. R 14 yrs Mar 1762 but pardoned for Army service same month. Ha.
Chiverson, Edward. S Bristol & TB to Md Apr 1767. G.
Christopher, John of St. Philip & Jacob. S Bristol Feb 1751 AT Apr 1752. G.
Chubb, Alexander. R to be T for life Apr 1772. K.
Churcher, Charles. R 14 yrs Jun 1765. Sx.
Churchill, Mary, singlewoman. S Bristol Sep 1745. G.
Clagharty, John. S Bristol May TB to Md Sep 1763. G.
Clansey, Elizabeth (1688). *See* Morris. M.
• Clapham, William. S Lent R Jly T Dec 1736 *Dorsetshire*. Ht.
• Clarke, Arthur. S Sep T 14 yrs Nov 1762 *Prince William*, removed from ship for examination as bankrupt; pardoned Oct 1763. M.
Clark, Elizabeth wife of William. S Bristol Apr 1741. G.
• Clark, James. S Bristol Apr R 14 yrs for plundering the *Hopewell* while she was stranded & TB to Va Jly 1772. G.
Clark, James. R 14 yrs (Bristol) Jun 1772

21

Clark, John. AT Bristol Aug 1741. G.
- Clarke, John. S Summer but pardoned for Army service Oct 1762. No.

Clarke, Richard. S Lent 1775. Bu.

Clarke, Robert of Erith. R for Barbados Jun 1671. K.

Clarke, Thomas of Watchet, husbandman. R for Barbados Jly 1671. So.
- Clark, Thomas. S Summer 1741 R Feb T 14 yrs Apr 1742 *Bond*. K.
- Clarke, Thomas. R Jun T Sep 1766 *Justitia*. K.
- Clark, Valentine. S Summer 1746 R 14 yrs Summer 1747. Cu.

Clarke, William of New Sarum, tailor. R for Barbados Feb 1671. Wi.
- Clark, William. R & TB 14 yrs Apr 1770 *New Trial* but pardoned for sea service Dec 1770. M.
- Claxton, Edward. S May 1721 R Jan T 14 yrs Jly 1722 *Alexander*. L.

Clayton, Thomas. S Summer T Oct 1763. Li.

Clement, Eleanor. S Bristol Mar 1738. G.
- Clement, Nathaniel. S Lent R 14 yrs May 1733. Ha.

Clements, Edward of Fulham. R Jun 1714 & to remain in Newgate until transported. M.
- Clements, Edward. S Lent R 14 yrs Jly 1724. Wi.
- Clifford, Edward. R & T for life Apr 1769 *Tryal*. K.

Clifford, Highgate. S Bristol Apr 1739. G.

Clifford, William. S Mar 1759 s heifer R 14 yrs Jun 1760. Ha.

Clift, John. S Bristol Feb 1753. G.
- Clift, Thomas. S May but taken from ship & pardoned Jly 1775. L.
- Clifton, Thomas. S Apr but R to serve in 49th Regiment in Jamaica Apr 1761. L.
- Clinch, William. S & TB Oct 1762 *Prince William* but pardoned same month. L.
- Clippingdale, George of Bristol. R for life for murder May 1763 after consenting to amputation of limb to test styptic. G.

Clivring, Peter (1769). *See* Williams, William. G.
- Clogg, Robert Jr. S Summer 1740 R 14 yrs Feb 1741. De.

Clough, John. S Bristol Apr R 14 yrs & TB to Va Jly 1772. G.

Coates, Francis Peachey. R to T himself for life for highway robbery Sep 1766. Sy.

Coatley, George. S Summer 1732 R May 1733. Be.
- Cock, Richard. S Summer 1733 for forgery R 14 yrs Jan 1734. Ha.

Cock, William. S Lent R May 1733. So.
- Cockley, William. S Jly 1758 R Feb T 14 yrs Apr 1759 *Thetis*. E.

Colbourne, Samuel. R Jun 1768. Do.

Collborn, Thomas. SQS Bristol Nov 1769 TB to Md May 1770. G.
- Cole, Francis. R Nov 1769 TB to Va 1770. De.

Cole, John. S Bristol Sep 1737. G.
- Cole, Richard. S Lent R Jun T 14 yrs Oct 1738 *Genoa*. Sy.
- Coleman, Edward. S Dec 1773 but pardoned same month. L.

Coleman, William. S Lent 1767. No.
Coles, James. S Bristol Apr 1745. G.
Coleshill, James. S Summer 1741 R 14 yrs Feb 1742. Bu.
- Collepriest, John. R 14 yrs Jan 1737. So.
- Collett, John. R Apr T Oct 1723 *Forward*. Sy.
Collett, Sarah, spinster. SQS Bristol Mar TB to Md Apr 1769. G.
Collingwood, Thomas. S Summer 1726 R Jun 1727. Li.
Collins, John. S Bristol Mar 1736. G.
Collins, John. S Bristol Aug 1749. G.
Collins, Rose, widow. S Bristol Jly 1733. G.
Collis, William (1762). *See* Collison. E.
- Collison *alias* Collis, William. TB Apr 1762 *Neptune* but pardoned for Army service in Jamaica same month. E.
Colliver, Shadrack. S for sacrilege Aug 1726 R Jly 1727. Co.
- Colson, William. S Lent 1744. No.
Coltman, Joseph. R to be T for life Nov 1773. Du.
- Colwell, Anne. S Lent as pickpocket R 14 yrs Jly 1726. De.
Combes, Alexander. S Bristol Feb 1741. G.
Condell, Lawrence. S Bristol Feb AT Aug 1749. G.
Connor, Eleanor. R 14 yrs (Bristol) Apr 1748. G.
Connor, Eleanor. R 14 yrs Bristol Aug 1748. G.
- Conner, Temperance wife of George. S as pickpocket Lent R 14 yrs Jun 1734. Co.
- Conroy, John [*not James*]. S Oct, case reviewed unfavourably Nov T Dec 1770 *Justitia*. M.
Conway, Patrick. S Bristol Aug 1725 to be tried at Gloucester for returning from T. G.
- Cook, John. S Apr TB *Tayloe*, respited May 1772. M.
Cooke, Joseph. SQS 14 yrs for receiving Jly 1773. Sh.
- Cook, Ralph. S 14 yrs s linen from bleaching croft at Osmotherly Summer TB Aug 1773; pardoned Aug 1774. Y.
- Cooke, Thomas, packer. S Jan TB *Tryal* but R to T himself Jan 1764. L.
- Cook, Thomas. S Apr-Jun TB *Tayloe* but pardoned Jun 1772. M.
- Cook, William. S Mar but pardoned Apr 1773. Ha.
Cooper, Edward of Epping. R for Barbados or Jamaica Mar 1709. E.
- Cooper, George. TB May 1767 *Thornton* but pardoned Sep 1767. M.
Cooper, George. SQS Bristol Mar TB to Va May 1775. G.
- Cooper, Henry. T *Expedition* from Bristol to South Carolina 1728. Wi.
- Cooper, John. R Apr T Oct 1723 *Forward*. E.
- Cooper, John. S Summer 1740 R Feb T 14 yrs Apr 1741 *Speedwell* or *Mediterranean*. E.
- Cooper, John. R Lent 1773 for rape but taken from ship to T himself for life Dec 1773. E.
- Cooper, Thomas. S Summer 1742 R 14 yrs Feb 1753. Do.

- Cooper, William. R Summer 1755 but pardoned for Army service May 1756. Ht.
Cope, John. S Bristol May 1761; to hang Oct 1761 for returning. G.
- Coping, Thomas. S Summer 1742 R Feb T 14 yrs Apr 1743 *Justitia* but died on passage. E.
- Corbet, Henry. S killing deer at Uttoxeter Lent but R for Army service in Jamaica Apr 1762. St.
- Courbé [*not Courby*], Peter of St. George, Hanover Square. S s handkerchief Sep 1740 but R to T himself for life Mar 1741. M.
- Cordozo, Jacob. S Dec 1742 R for life Apr 1743. M.
- Cordosa, Jacob. SQS Dec 1770 TB *Thornton* but R for sea service same month. M.
- Corke, Arthur. S Aug 1764 R Feb T 14 yrs Apr 1765 *Ann*. Sx.
- Cornbury, Richard. S Sep-Dec 1755 TB Jan 1756 *Greyhound* but pardoned same month. M.
Cornelius, Lawrence. R 7 yrs Feb 1767. Ha.
Cornell, John (1760). *See* Cornhill. St.
- Cornhill *alias* Cornell, John. S Summer 1760 R 14 yrs Lent 1761 TB *Atlas* from Bristol but R for Army service Aug 1761. St.
- Corpe, Richard. S Jan pardoned Feb 1773. M.
Costen, Gawen, mariner. S Bristol Nov 1740. G.
- Cotterell, Nicholas of Lambeth. SQS Feb 1757; pardoned to return from Md Apr 1758. Sy.
- Cottle, Ann wife of James. SQS 14 yrs Bristol Aug 1771 TB to Va Jly 1772. G.
- Cottle, Grant. S Bristol Apr R for life & TB to Va Jun 1771. G.
Coultas, William, yeoman. SQS Hull Dec 1758 TB Jan 1759. Y.
Coverdale, Thomas. R 14 yrs Jun 1768. Ha.
- Coward, James. S May 1771 TB *Scarsdale* but pardoned same month. L.
Coward, Margaret of St. Paul Covent Garden, spinster. R for Barbados or Jamaica Aug 1700. M.
Cradock, John. S (Bristol) Feb 1724. G.
- Crain, Jasper. S Summer 1740 R Feb T 14 yrs Apr 1741 *Speedwell* or *Mediterranean*. Ht.
- Cran *alias* Crandon, Abraham. S Lent R 14 yrs Jly 1724. Do.
Crandon, Abraham (1724). *See* Cran. Do.
Crawford, Richard. R 14 yrs Bristol Sep 1748. G.
- Cripps *alias* Peeke, John. R 14 yrs Aug 1760 but pardoned to serve in Army Aug 1761. So.
- Crispin, Alexander. R Nov 1769 TB to Va 1770. De.
Crocker, James. S Summer 1741 R 14 yrs Feb 1742. De.
- Crook, Francis. S Aug 1764 TB *Justitia* but pardoned same month. L.
Croome, Thomas of Longbridge Deverill, broadweaver. R for America Jly 1696. Wi.

Cross, Frances, spinster. SQS Bristol Feb TB to Va Aug 1774. G.
Cross, William. S Bristol Sep 1745. G.
Crotch, Edward. S Summer 1741 R 14 yrs Feb 1742. Nf.
Croughton, John. R 14 yrs Feb 1766 s sheep. O.
Crow, Sarah, singlewoman. S Bristol Aug AT Sep 1741. G.
Crow, William, cordwainer. S (Bury St. Edmunds) Nov 1770. Su.
Crowforth, John. R for life for riotous assembly in Norwich Feb 1767. Nf.
- Crowhurst, John. R Jly T 14 yrs Sep 1764 *Justitia*. K.
Crutchfield, Peter. R for Barbados May 1664. L.
- Cryer, William. S & R & T 14 yrs Jan 1722 *Gilbert* LC Annapolis Jly 1722. M.
Cudd, Ann. S Bristol Nov 1748. G.
Cudmore, William of Crediton, Devon. S Bristol to be hanged for returning from T Apr 1752. G.
Cuffe, Peter. R 14 yrs Bristol Mar 1741. G.
Cullen, Andrew. R for counterfeiting May 1728. So.
Cullin, Charles. S Bristol Mar 1738. G.
- Culmore, Joseph of Rotherhithe. SQS Jan TB *Ann* but pardoned Mar 1765. Sy.
Cumley, Benjamin. S Bristol Aug 1758. G.
Cummings, Richard. R Jun 1714 & to remain in Newgate until transported. L.
Cunningham, Thomas of York Castle. R for Africa or America Jly 1715. Y.
Cunningham, Thomas of St. Thomas's. S Bristol Jun 1752. G.
Cunningham, William (1773). *See* Orr. Nl.
Cunningham, William Sr., aged 61, wool card maker. S Apr 1775 but in Morpeth Prison in Dec 1775. Nl.
Cunningham, William Jr., aged 24, tinker. S Apr 1775 but in Morpeth Prison in Dec 1775. Nl.
Cure, William. SQS Bristol Mar TB to Md Apr 1767. G.
Curley, Edward. S 14 yrs Bristol Jun AT Aug 1749 but then pardoned. G.
Curry, Sarah, spinster. SQS Bristol & TB May 1769 LC Rappahannock from *Brickdale* as Sarah Corrie Aug 1769. G.
Curtess, Richard (1756). *See* Curtis. Nl.
Curtis, Margaret wife of Joseph. SQS Bristol Mar TB to Va Apr 1773. G.
- Curtis, Mary. S for murder Summer 1740 R Feb T 14 yrs Apr 1741 *Speedwell* or *Mediterranean*. E.
- Curtis *alias* Curtess, Richard. S Aug 1756 for murder R for life Sep 1757. Nl.
Curtis, William. S Bristol to hang for returning from T Mar 1742. G.
Cuss, Robert. R 14 yrs Apr 1771. G.

- Cuthbert, James. S Sep-Oct to be T 14 yrs but taken from ship & pardoned Dec 1773. M.
- Cuthbertson, John. S Apr but pardoned for Army service May 1761. M.

- Dagger, Mary. S for murder Summer 1743 R Feb T 14 yrs May 1744 *Justitia*. Sy.

Dancey, John. S Summer 1740 R 14 yrs Feb 1741. St.

Daniel, John. S Bristol Dec 1750. G.

- Daniel, John. SQS Bristol Jan 1767, taken from ship on appeal Aug but sentence confirmed Oct 1767 TB to Md Apr 1768. G.
- Darby, Edmund. S s sheep & R 14 yrs Summer but pardoned Sep 1775. St.

Darlington *alias* Dartiston, John. R Jly 1769. Fl.

Dartiston, John (1769). *See* Darlington. Fl.

David, Thomas. R (Chester Circuit) for Barbados Nov 1666. X.

Davie, William. SQS Bristol May TB to Va Jun 1771. G.

Davis, David. S Bristol Dec 1736. G.

Davis, Edward. SQS Bristol Feb TB to Md Apr 1765. G.

Davis, Eleanor. S Apr R Jly 1752. St.

- Davis, Hezekiah of Little Sodbury. R for parts overseas Jly 1717. G.

Davies, James. S Bristol Jan AT Feb 1743. G.

Davis, James. SQS Bristol Feb TB to Md Apr 1769. G.

Davis, Jane wife of William, pedlar. S Bristol Feb 1735. G.

Davis, Jane. SQS Bristol Aug 1760 TB to Md Apr 1761. G.

Davis, John. S Bristol Aug 1739. G.

Davis, John. SQS Bristol Jan TB to Md Apr 1768. G.

Davies, John. R 14 yrs Sep 1768. Ha.

Davis *alias* Carroll, John. S Bristol & TB to Va Apr 1773. G.

Davis, Mary. S Summer 1742 R 14 yrs Feb 1743. K.

Davis, Mary, singlewoman. S Bristol Oct 1747. G.

- Davis, Mary. S May-Jly TB Sep *Greyhound* but pardoned Oct 1751. M.

Davis, Philip. R 14 yrs Bristol Aug 1755. G.

- Davis, Philip of Bristol. R 14 yrs Aug 1773 but pardoned Oct 1774. G.
- Davis, Richard. S Lent R 14 yrs Jun 1746. De.
- Davis, Robert. S Apr TB *Tryal* but pardoned for sea service May 1758. M.
- Davies, Samuel of Astley Abbotts. R for parts overseas Jly 1719. Sh.
- Davis, Sarah. S Bristol May TB to Md Sep 1763. G.
- Davis, Thomas. S Summer 1741 R Feb T 14 yrs Apr 1742 *Bond*. Ht.

Davis, Thomas. SQS Bristol Nov 1767 TB to Md Apr 1768. G.

- Davies, Thomas. S s yarn at Baschurch Summer but pardoned Sep 1774. Sh.

Davis, Velvidera, singlewoman. S Bristol Aug AT Sep 1741. G.

Davis, William of Newbury, glover. R for America Jly 1696. Be.
Davis, William. R Jun 1714 & to remain in Newgate until transported. L.
Davis, William. S Bristol May 1751. G.
• Davis, William. S Lent but R to serve in 49th Regiment in Jamaica Apr 1761. Sy.
Davis, William. SQS Bristol Mar TB to Va May 1774. G.
Davison, Phebe (1774). *See* Maeks. Nl.
Davy, John. R 14 yrs Apr 1769. So.
Davy, Margaret. SQS Bristol Feb TB to Md Apr 1767. G.
Davy, Philip. S Bristol Jun 1750. G.
• Dawson, Joseph of St. Thomas, Southwark. SQS Jan TB *Thornton* but pardoned Feb 1768. Sy.
• Day, Benjamin. R & T for life Apr 1770 *New Trial*. Sy.
Day, John. SQS Hull Sep 1749. Y.
Day, John. SL Mar T Apr 1753 *Thames*. Sy.
• Day, John. R & T for life Apr 1770 *New Trial*. Ht.
Day, Mary, widow. S Bristol Feb 1753. G.
• Day, Richard. S Summer 1750 R 14 yrs Feb 1751. So.
Day, Thomas. R for life Apr 1770. Ht.
• Dayly *alias* Peterson, John, *alias* Gahogan, Walter. S & T for life Sep 1755 *Tryal*; found at large but pardoned Jly 1766. L.
Deal, William. R Apr 1725. K.
Deane, George of Lambeth. R for Barbados Jun 1671. Sy.
• Deans, Jane. S Jan TB *Tryal* but removed from ship & pardoned Feb 1764. M.
Dearlove, William Sr. of Owthorne. SQS Beverley Easter 1772. Y.
Dearlove, William of Leathorne(?). SQS Beverley 1774. Y.
• Debart, Joseph. R May T 14 yrs Sep 1767 *Justitia*. E.
Dee, Thomas. R 14 yrs Feb 1766 s horse. O.
Deeble, Joseph (1746). *See* Hatch. De.
• Deeley, Mary. T *Expedition* from Bristol to South Carolina 1728. Wo.
Deere, Richard of Castle Combe, husbandman. R for America Jly 1696. Wi.
• Dekin, Thomas. SL Nov TB *Neptune* but pardoned Nov 1763. Sy.
Delafountaine, Peter. S for issuing forged note, T respited for his relations in Holland to provide a comfortable voyage Jan 1747 L.
Delafountain, Peter. R to T himself for life for forgery Sep 1762. L.
Denham, Joseph. S Bristol Dec 1750. G.
Dennis, John, mariner. S Bristol Feb 1735. G.
Dennison, George. S Bristol Aug 1747 s tankard R 14 yrs Aug 1748. G.
• Dennison, Michael. S 14 yrs for receiving Aug; to T himself Dec 1774. Co.
Densley, Arthur. S Aug 1757 R 14 yrs Feb 1758. De.
Densley, Joseph. SQS Bristol Dec 1765 TB to Md Apr 1766. G.

- Denton *alias* Holland, Ann of St. Giles in Fields, spinster. R for America May 1704. M.
- Derham, Abraham. R Apr 1759. De.
- Derreck, Richard. S Winter 1735 R Jun 1736. So.
- Derricott, Mary. S Bristol May 1747. G.
- Devourex, Richard of Finchley. R for Barbados Sep 1677. M.
- Dew, Henry Jr. SQS Lent 1770. O.
- Dew, John. S Summer 1733 R 14 yrs Jun 1734. Ha.
- Diaper, John. S Jan-Feb TB *Thornton* but pardoned Mar 1771. M.
- Dibley, Thomas. S Lent R 14 yrs Jun TB to Va Sep 1744. Wi.
- Dickery, William. S Lent R Jly 1724. So.
- Dickie, James. S for assaulting Customs officer on Holy Island Summer 1765 but pardoned Mar 1766. Du.
- Dickinson, George. SQS Hull Epiphany 1774. Y.
- Dickinson, Rebecca (1701). *See* Mound. M.
- Dickinson, William Jr. of Great Kelk, husbandman. SQS Beverley Summer 1741. Y.
- Diddle *alias* Britten, William. SQS Bristol Dec 1769 TB to Md May 1770. G.
- Digsby, George. R on petition of inhabitants of Hoddesdon Apr T Oct 1723 *Forward*. Ht.
- Diggle, Joseph of Birtle, carpenter. S for forgery Lent R 14 yrs Summer 1769; found at large & pardoned Jly 1774. La.
- Dillon, Theobald. SQS Bristol Sep 1767 TB to Md Apr 1768. G.
- Dimmock, William. S Jly 1765 R 14 yrs Feb 1766. Ht.
- Dinham, Joseph (1746). *See* Hatch. De.
- Dinnick *alias* Tredinnick, William. S Summer 1752 R Feb 1753. De.
- Dixey, Elizabeth. S Bristol Mar 1765. G.
- Dixon, Elizabeth. S Bristol Mar TB to Md Apr 1765. G.
- Dixon, John. S Summer 1729 R Feb T Sep 1730 *Smith*. Sy.
- Dixon, John. S Lent R Jun T 14 yrs Oct 1738 *Genoa*. Sy.
- Dixon, John. R & T for life Apr 1770 *New Trial*. K.
- Dickson, Silas. R for life Apr 1774. Db.
- Divison, Samuel. S Lent R Jun 1724. Li.
- Dobson, John. SQS Hull Epiphany 1752. Y.
- Dobson, Thomas. S Lent R Jun T Jly 1724 *Robert*. Sy.
- Dobson, Thomas. R for life May 1765. Ca.
- Dodd, William, weaver. S Bristol Nov 1739. G.
- Dodson, Jonathan. SQS Hull Epiphany 1754. Y.
- Dollings, Sarah, singlewoman. S Bristol Aug 1739. G.
- Domini, Thomas. R Jun 1768. Ha.
- Donkan, William. S Summer 1746 R 14 yrs Summer 1747; found at large & S to hang Summer 1751. Y.
- Donkin, William. SQS Hull Easter 1774. Y.
- Donnolly, John. S Feb TB Apr *Ann* but pardoned Jly 1766. M.

Donovan, Eleanor, widow. S Bristol Aug 1753. G.
- Dorling [*not Darling*], Mones. S for forgery Summer 1762 R for life Feb 1763. Su.

Dorricott, Richard SQS Lent 1774. Sh.

Douglass, William Sr. S as pickpocket Lent R Jun 1727. Nt.
- Douglas, William. TB *Dolphin*, respited Apr 1764. K.

Dovey, Walter Burne (1759). *See* Landovery. G.
- Dowdell, William. S Jan TB Apr *Dolphin* but R for Army service Oct 1761. L.

Down, James. S Bristol Mar 1751. G.

Downing, Solomon. S Lent R Jun 1724. Li.
- Downing, William Biron. S Lent R 14 yrs Jly 1754. K.
- Doyle, Michael. SQS Jun TB *Justitia* but pardoned Aug 1767. M.

Drake, Bamfylde. R 14 yrs Jun 1758. Ha.

Drake, Edward. SQS Bristol & TB to Md Aug 1769. G.

Drakes, William. SQS Hull Epiphany TB Jan 1770. Y.

Drehlen, Stephen. S Bristol Apr 1752. G.

Drew, Richard of Okehampton, blacksmith. R for America Jly 1696. De.

Driver, Hester. S Bristol May TB to Md Sep 1766 LC Annapolis from *Randolph* Mar 1767. G.
- Driver, John. S s cloth from tenters Summer 1726 R Jun T Sep 1727 *Forward* LC Rappahannock May 1728. No.

Drossitt, Mary. S for shoplifting Lent R Jun 1723. Bd.

Dry, Samuel (or John). SQS Hull Easter 1756. Y.

Duck, Peter of Ashfield. R Jly 1703. Su.
- Dudson, John. T *Expedition* from Bristol to South Carolina 1728. Wi.

Dugmore, John. S Summer 1764 R 14 yrs Jun 1765; found at large & R for life Jun 1766. K.

Dunford, Patrick. SQS Bristol Oct 1770 TB to Va Mar 1771. G.

Dunn, Elizabeth, wife of John of St. Saviour Southwark. R for Barbados or Jamaica Mar 1709. Sy.

Dunn, Isabel. S Bristol Sep 1731. G.

Dunn, William. S Bristol Feb AT Apr 1745. G.
- Dunning, Alexander. S Oct but taken from ship & pardoned Nov 1773. L.

Dunny, William. S Bristol Oct 1749. G.
- Dunton, John. Respited Aug 1718 R 14 yrs Lent T May 1719 *Margaret* LC Md May 1720; sold to John Amslow. Sy.

Durham, Ann. R 14 yrs Feb 1764. Ht.
- Durham, John. R Jun T 14 yrs Sep 1765 *Justitia*. Sy.
- Durnford, Ambrose. S Lent 1727 R 14 yrs Feb 1731. Wi.

Dutton, William. S Bristol May TB to Md Sep 1763. G.

Dyde, Michael (1766). *See* Dye. M.
- Dye *alias* Dyde, Michael. SQS Dec 1766 TB Jan 1767 *Tryal* but pardoned Sep 1767. M.

Dyer, Anthony of Fulham. R for Barbados or Jamaica Mar 1688. M.
- Dyer *alias* Latouch *alias* Massey, Mary of St. Martin in Fields, spinster. R Aug AT Oct 1701. M.

Dyer, Peter. SQS Bristol Mar TB to Md Apr 1766. G.

Dyer, Thomas of Martock, husbandman. R for Barbados Jly 1671. So.

- Eades, George. S Sep TB *Neptune* but pardoned Nov 1767. M.

Eades, James, butcher. S Bristol Sep 1734. G.

Eaglefield, Thomas of Derby[shire]. R for America Feb 1696. Db.

Eaman, Thomas. SQS Hull Epiphany TB Feb 1766. Y.

Earle, Paul SQS Lent 1770. G.

Eashall, Thomas of St. Margaret Westminster. R for Barbados or Jamaica Aug 1700. M.

East, Anne, singlewoman. S Bristol Dec 1740. G.

- East *alias* Wiggington, John. SQS Dec 1772 but taken from ship & pardoned Mar 1773. M.
- Eaton, Ann. S Sep-Oct but taken from ship & pardoned Nov 1772. M.
- Eddy, Patrick. S Jly but R for Army or Navy Aug 1761. Co.

Edhouse, Elizabeth wife of Samuel. S (Bury St. Edmunds) Lent 1773. Su.

Edmonds, William. R 14 yrs Feb 1767. K.

Edwards, Ann. SQS Bristol May TB to Md Sep 1766 LC Annapolis from *Randolph* Mar 1767. G.

Edwards *alias* Williams, Charles. R 14 yrs Apr 1769. So.

Edwards, James. SQS Bristol Nov 1769 TB to Md May 1770. G.

Edwards, John. S Lent R Jly 1736. Sy.

Edwards, John. S Bristol Apr 1743. G.

Edwards, John. S Bristol Feb 1751. G.

- Edwards, Mary, aged 13. S & TB Mar *Neptune* but taken from ship & pardoned Apr 1763. L.

Edwards, Robert of Cambridge. R Jly 1703. Ca.

Edwards, William. S Bristol Sep 1751. G.

- Edwick, Elizabeth. S Lent R Jly T Dec 1736 *Dorsetshire*. E.
- Egbear, William. S Mar R 14 yrs Jly 1758. De.

Eldridge, Jane, singlewoman. S Bristol Sep 1746. G.

- Eldridge, John. R & T 14 yrs Apr 1770 *New Trial*. Sy.
- Eleazer, Jacob. S for perjury Oct T 14 yrs Dec 1771 *Justitia*; respited on appeal of Henry E. Dec 1771. L.
- Eling, Samuel, a youth. R Aug 1737 T for life Jun 1738 *Forward*. Sy.

Ellery, Betty. SQS Bristol May 1766 TB to Md Apr 1767. G.

- Elligoe, William of Greetham. R for America Feb 1713 & Jun 1714. Ru.
- Elliott, Christopher [*not* Edward]. R for America Aug 1715. L.

30

- Elliott, John. S Jan TB *Dolphin* but R for Army service Dec 1761. L.
- Elliott, Robert. S Jly TB 14 yrs *Justitia* but pardoned Aug 1766. M.

Elliott, Stephen of St. Margaret Westminster. R for Barbados or Jamaica Aug 1700. M.
- Ellis, John. R May T 14 yrs Sep 1767 *Justitia*. Sy.
- Ellis, Joseph. S Lent R May 1731 TB to Va. De.

Ellis, William. S Mar 1759 R 14 yrs Jun 1760. Ha.
- Ellis, William. S Jly 1760 TB to Va but R for Army service Jly 1761. De.

Elmes, John of Lacock, tucker. R for America Jly 1696. Wi.

Elsley, Matthew of Fulham. R for Barbados Sep 1677. M.
- Elsom, Robert. R Jan T Feb 1726 *Supply* LC Annapolis May 1726. K.
- Emblen, James. S Oct 1761 but R for Army service same month. L.
- Emery, George. S Lent 1747 but pardoned for Army service in Gibraltae May 1748. Bd.

Emmerson, Barbara. SQS Hull Epiphany 1754. Y.
- Ends, Elizabeth. T *Expedition* from Bristol to South Carolina 1728. Wi.

England, Isaac. R 14 yrs Nov 1769 TB to Va 1770. De.

English, Ann. SL Aug T Oct 1760 *Phoenix*. Sy.
- Erith, Jeffery of Belchamp St. Paul, victualler. SQS Jan TB *Thetis* but taken from ship & pardoned Apr 1759. E.
- Erouselle, Philip. S Jun TB *Douglas* but pardoned Jun 1769. L.
- Erskine *alias* Maxwell *alias* Hamilton, Thomas. S Jan-Feb TB *Thornton* but R to T himself Mar 1771. M.

Erskine, William. R to T himself 7 yrs Nov 1773. L or M.

Esbury, James. SQS Lent 1773. G.

Evan, Jenkin. R (Chester Circuit) for Barbados Nov 1666. X.
- Evans, Elizabeth. S & TB Apr *Tryal* but pardoned Jun 1769. L.
- Evans, George. R Apr T for life Dec 1771 *Justitia*. Sy.
- Evans, John. T *Expedition* from Bristol to South Carolina 1728. G.
- Evans, John. R 14 yrs Jun but pardoned for sea service Sep 1761. Ha.
- Evans *alias* Burges, John. S s pigs at Enville Lent but taken from ship & pardoned Jly 1773. St.

Evans, Lewis. S Bristol Sep 1731. G.
- Evans, Margaret. S as pickpocket Lent R 14 yrs May 1733. Ha.

Evans, Richard. R for Barbados May 1664. L.

Evemy, Samuel. S Summer 1741 R 14 yrs Feb 1742. Do.

Evered, Robert, mariner. R (Bristol) for Barbados Jan 1681. G.

Everett, Richard. S 14 yrs Bristol & TB to Md Apr 1764. G.
- Everett, William. S Dec 1761 TB *Dolphin* but R for Army service Jan 1762. M.

Evy, Thomas. S Summer 1740 R 14 yrs Feb 1741. Ht.

Ewen, Robert. S Lent R 14 yrs Jun 1744. Ha.

Ewer, Edward. S Bristol Aug 1733. G.

- Facer, Joseph. S Summer but R for Army service in Jamaica Oct 1762. No.
Fare, John. S Bristol Apr 1752. G.
- Farley, Ann. S 14 yrs for receiving goods stolen at Castlemorton Lent but pardoned May 1759. Wo.
Farley, Elizabeth. SQS Bristol Aug TB to Md Oct 1762. G.
- Farley, John. S Aug 1764 R Feb T 14 yrs Apr 1765 *Ann.* Sx.
Farrell *alias* Forrel, James. R 14 yrs Sep 1768. Ha.
Farrell, John. S Bristol Mar 1753. G.
- Farrin [*not Farrie*], John. S Lent R Jly T Dec 1734 *Caesar.* E.
- Farthing, Samuel. S Lent R Jun 1734. So.
Faucett, Thomas. S Summer 1746 R 14 yrs Jly 1747. Y.
Fear, Catherine. S Bristol Apr 1751. G.
Featherstone, Elizabeth (1724). *See* Levingstone. Ha.
Featherstonehaugh, Timothy. R to T himself 7 yrs Jly 1774. L.
- Fellows, Thomas. SQS Jly 1769 but pardoned same month. M.
Felton, Jeremiah. SQS Bristol Apr TB to Md May 1770. G.
Fenley, John. SQS Summer 1765. Nt.
Fenton, Barbara wife of Henry of Hull, flaxdresser. SQS Hull Dec 1758 TB Jan 1759. Y.
- Fenton, William. S Apr TB *Scarsdale* but pardoned Jly 1770. L.
- Ferguson, John. S Sep but R for Army service Oct 1761. M.
Fest, Robert of Wincanton. R for America Jly 1696. So.
- Fettiplace, George. S Sep, case reviewed unfavourably & T Dec 1770 *Justitia.* M.
Fewtrell, Charles (1723). *See* Bore.
Fey, William. S Mar R 14 yrs Jly 1757. Sx.
Field, John. R for life Feb 1767. G.
- Field, John. R Sep T 14 yrs Dec 1771 *Justitia.* Ht.
- Fielder, John of Winford. S Lent for forging land tax receipt R 14 yrs May 1744. So.
Filming, William (1762). *See* Fleming. La.
- Findme *alias* Foundme, Peter. S Lent R 14 yrs Jly 1724. Ha.
- Finnick, Francis. S Oct TB *Justitia* but pardoned Nov 1769. L.
Fire, Michael. S Bristol Mar 1741. G.
- Fish, Thomas. R 14 yrs s salt from warehouse Jun 1736. Ha.
Fishe, William of Whitsondine. R for America Jun 1714. Ru.
- Fisher, Hannah, spinster. S Bristol Apr R 14 yrs & TB to Va May 1774. G.
- Fisher, Margaret. R Sep T Oct 1722 *Forward* LC Annapolis Jun 1723. M.
Fisher, Mary, spinster, *alias* wife of John of St. Saviour Southwark. R for Barbados Jun 1671. Sy.
Fitchet, William. S Bristol Sep 1728 T *Expedition* from Bristol to South Carolina. G.

- Fitzgerald, Andrew. R Dec 1765 T for life Apr 1766 *Ann*. L.
Fitzgerald, William. S Bristol Nov 1730. G.
- Flack, John. S s hog at Pampisford Lent but pardoned Mar 1773. Ca.
Flaming, William (1762). *See* Fleming. La.
- Flathers, Benjamin of St. Paul Covent Garden. SW Jun 1775 but pardoned same month. M.
Flaxon, Richard. S Lent s horse R May 1733. G.
Fleming *alias* Keeling, Joseph. R Jun 1737. Ht.
- Fleming *alias* Flaming *alias* Filming, William of Manchester, innholder. S for perjury Lent 1761 R for life Feb 1762. La.
Fletcher, George. SQS s ox chain Jly 1772. Sh.
- Fletcher, Joseph, recruit to Regiment of Foot. S s at Market Drayton Lent but pardoned Apr 1748. Sh.
- Fletcher, Samuel, recruit to Regiment of Foot. S s at Market Drayton Lent but pardoned Apr 1748. Sh.
- Fletcher, William. R Jly T for life Dec 1734 *Caesar* LC Va Jly 1735. M.
Flindall, Joseph. R for life Jan 1772. L.
- Flinders, William. S Lent T Apr 1758 *Lux* from London. Db.
- Flinn, Barnard. S Jan TB *Dolphin* but pardoned Jan 1762. M.
- Flint, Richard. S Jan-Feb but taken from ship & pardoned Apr 1775. M.
- Flood, John. S Summer 1740 R Feb T 14 yrs Apr 1741 *Speedwell* or *Mediterranean*. Sy.
Flood, Samuel. S Bristol & TB to Md Apr 1767. G.
Flower, Elizabeth, spinster, *alias* wife of John of St. Saviour Southwark. R for Barbados Jun 1671. Sy.
Flower, John. S (Bristol) Aug 1723. G.
- Fogg *alias* Trigg, John. R Apr T 14 yrs Oct 1723 *Forward*. E.
- Foler, Robert. S Jan but taken from ship & pardoned Apr 1774. L.
Folkes, William. S Bristol Dec 1751. G.
Follin, Margaret, singlewoman. S Bristol Feb AT Mar 1742. G.
- Folliot [*not Follitt*], William. S Feb TB *Neptune* but pardoned same month. L.
- Fooks, Robert. S Mar but pardoned to serve at sea May 1756. Do.
- Foot, Esau. R & T 14 yrs Apr 1769 *Tryal*. Sy.
- Foot, George. S Summer 1734 R 14 yrs Feb 1735. Do.
Ford, John. S Bristol May AT Aug 1753. G.
Forrel, James (1768). *See* Farrell. Ha.
- Forsith, John, *alias* Berkley, William. R & T for life Apr 1769 *Tryal*. Sy.
Fosker, William (1774). *See* Foster. M.
- Fossett, Edward. S Sep but pardoned Oct 1774. M.
- Foster, Edward. S Mar 1761 but pardoned for sea service same month. L.
Foster, Richard. S Summer 1759 R 14 yrs Lent 1760. Li.
Foster, Samuel. S Bristol Sep 1728. G.

- Forster, Robert, *alias* Bell, William. S Summer 1746 R 14 yrs Summer 1747. Nl.

  Foster, Samuel. S Bristol Sep 1728 T *Expedition* from Bristol to South Carolina. G.
- Foster *alias* Fosker, William of St. Paul Covent Garden. SW Apr 1774. M.

  Foundme, Peter (1724). *See* Findme. Ha.
- Fowke, Sarah. S Lent T Apr 1757 *Lux* from London. Db.

  Fowler, Elizabeth wife of David. S for receiving feather bed T 14 yrs Jun TB TB *Dolphin* but pardoned Aug 1764. M.

  Fowles, John. S Bristol May TB to Md Sep 1766 LC Annapolis from *Randolph* as John Volles Mar 1767. G.

  Fox, Abraham (1770). *See* Fox, Owen. M.
- Fox, John. S Summer 1741 R Feb T 14 yrs Apr 1742 *Bond*. Sy.
- Fox, Owen *alias* Abraham. S 14 yrs for receiving goods stolen in Essex May but pardoned Jun 1770. M.
- Fox, William. R Apr T 14 yrs Dec 1771 *Justitia*. Sy.
- Frampton, Moses. S Summer 1752 R 14 yrs Mar 1753. Do.
- France, Henry. S Summer 1746 R 14 yrs Summer 1747. Y.
- Francis, Andrew. S s mare Lent R 14 yrs Summer 1733. Li.
- Francis, Christopher, mariner. S Bristol for s from *Hopewell* in distress R 14 yrs & TB to Va Apr 1773. G.
- Francis *alias* French, John. SQS Jun but pardoned Jly 1761. M.
- Francis, John. R Apr T 14 yrs Dec 1771 *Justitia*. E.
- Francis, Phebe. S Apr but pardoned May 1773. M.
- Francis, Samuel. S Dec 1760 but removed from *Neptune* & pardoned. M.

  Francois, Thomas. R 14 yrs Feb 1764. Ha.

  Frankland, William. R to T himself for life for a shooting Mar 1774. L.
- Frazer, Charlotte. Respited May 1764 TB *Dolphin* but pardoned same month. Sy.

  Frazier, Hugh. S for highway robbery Lent R Jun 1727. Li.

  Freame, Richard. SQS Bristol & TB to Va Sep 1773. G.

  Free, Thomas. S Summer 1743 R 14 yrs Feb 1744. So.

  Freeman, Thomas. S for shoplifting Lent R Jun 1727. Li

  Freise, John. S Mar 1730 R May 1731. Co.

  French, John (1761). *See* Francis. M.
- Friend, John. S Bristol Apr R 14 yrs & TB to Va Jun 1771. G.

  Frost, William (1715). *See* Williams. M.

  Froud, James. R for life Oct 1770. Sy.
- Fry, Richard. S Feb but taken from ship & pardoned Apr 1775. M.

  Fry, Samuel, hallier. S Bristol Mar 1736. G.

  Fry, Thomas. SQS Bristol May TB to Md Sep 1766 LC Annapolis from *Randolph* Mar 1767. G.
- Fryer, John. S Lent R 14 yrs Jun 1744 TB to Va 1745. De.
- Fullagate, Edward. R Jly T 14 yrs Nov 1762 *Prince William*. Sy.

- Fuller, Turpin. S Summer 1741 R Feb T 14 yrs Apr 1742 *Bond*. E.
Furlong, Peter. S (Bristol) Feb 1723. G.
Fyson, Edward. S Gt. Yarmouth & R 14 yrs Sep 1761. Nf.
Fyson, Thomas (1747). *See* Lennon. E.

Gahogan, Walter (1755). *See* Dayly, John. L.
Gaine, Mary of St. Nicholas, spinster. S Bristol Mar AT Apr 1752. G.
Gainsford, William of Dymock. R for Barbados Oct 1663. G.
Galloway, John. R 14 yrs Bristol May 1743. G.
Galloway, William (1760). *See* Gallyford. De.
- Gallyford *alias* Galloway, William. S Jly 1760 TB to Va but pardoned to serve in Army Aug 1761. De.
- Gamble, John. S Mar TB to Va Apr 1768 but pardoned same month. Le.
Garbitt, John, trowman. S Bristol Jun 1735. G.
Gard, Charles. S Bristol Apr 1746. G.
Gardiner, Luke. S Bristol Mar TB to Md Apr 1765. G.
Gardner, Nicholas. R 14 yrs Bristol Oct 1740. G.
Garland, Joseph (1750). *See* Rainbird. K.
Garner, William. S Lent R Jun 1727. Li.
- Garnett, John. SL Jan 1773 [*not 1733*]. Sy.
- Garth, James. S s sheep at Marrick Lent R 14 yrs Summer TB Aug 1766; Elizabeth Garth pardoned Apr 1766. Y.
Garton, Robert of Nafferton. SQS Beverley Summer 1772. Y.
Gaskyn, Andrew of Exeter. R for America Jly 1696. De.
Gaskyns, Henry. R 14 yrs Jun 1768. So.
- Gason, William. S Lent but R for Army service Apr 1761. E.
- Gatfield, Robert. SWK Oct 1775 but pardoned same month. K.
- Gawen [*not Gowen*], Thomas of Shadwell. S Sep 1715 R & T Dec 1716 *Lewis* to Jamaica. M.
- Geare, Henry. S Nov 1761 TB *Prince William* but R for Navy Jly 1762. L.
Geary, Anthony. R Jun 1714 & to remain in Newgate until transported. L.
- Geary, Elizabeth. S Summer 1739 R Feb T Jun 1740 *Essex*. K.
Gee, Richard. S Lent R May 1731. De.
Genge, William of West Stafford. R for America Jly 1696. Do.
- Gibbons, Samuel. S Aug 1757 R Feb T 14 yrs Sep 1758 *Tryal* but taken from ship. Sy.
Gibbs, Jacob. S Bristol Dec 1736. G.
Gibbs, Thomas of Stangate. R for Barbados Jly 1671. Co.
Gibson, Elizabeth of St. Mary Savoy, spinster. R for Barbados Sep 1677. M.
Gibson, Thomas of Hollym. SQS Beverley Christmas 1769. Y.

Gilbert, Henry. S Bristol Aug 1743. G.
Gilbert, Nathaniel. R 14 yrs Jun 1768. Co.
Gilborne, Christian, spinster, *alias* wife of John of Clerkenwell. R for Barbados May 1664. M.
Gyles, John of Newington. R for Barbados Jun 1671. Sy.
Giles, Thomas, *alias* Chambers, William. R for life for highway robbery Sep 1747. E.
- Gilgore [*not Gilgose*], Francis. R 14 yrs Mar 1761 TB to Va. De.
Gill, Richard. S Bristol Sep 1735. G.
- Gill *alias* Bass, William, *alias* Taylor, George, *alias* Barber, Samuel. R s horse Lent 1761; found at large but pardoned Oct 1765. Le.
Gill, William. S Bristol Apr TB to Md Sep 1767. G.
Gillaboo, John. S Bristol Apr 1771. G.
Gillman, Samuel. S (Bury St. Edmunds) Summer 1766. Su.
- Gladmin [*not Gladwin*], John. S Mar R Jun T 14 yrs Dec 1758 *The Brothers*. Ht.
Glegg, Rebecca. SQS Hull Easter 1752. Y.
Glover, Edward. S Summer 1742 R 14 yrs Feb 1743. Sy.
Godby, John. S Bristol Sep 1741. G.
Godfrey, Anthony. S Lent R Jun 1724. Li.
- Godfrey *alias* Henry, John. R Aug but pardoned Sep 1773. Do.
- Godfrey, Thomas. R Jly for rape T for life Nov 1762 *Prince William*. E.
Godfrey, William. S Summer 1764 R 14 yrs Jan 1765. K.
Godwyn, Mary (1671). *See* Jenkins. So.
Going, Richard (1737). *See* Liveings. G.
- Goldring, Thomas. S Mar R Jun T 14 yrs Dec 1758 *The Brothers*. Sx.
Gonstan, George (1743). *See* Johnson. Y.
Goodall, Charles. R Jun 1714 & to remain in Newgate until transported. L.
Goodall, Richard SQS Lent 1770. O.
Goode, Edward of Tempsford. R for Barbados Jan 1665. Bd.
Goodfellow, Mathew. S Bristol Apr 1752. G.
Goodman, William. S Summer 1726 R Jun 1727. No.
- Goodson, Catherine. S Jly TB *Justitia* but pardoned Sep 1767. M.
Gopell, Dorothy Louisa. SQS Oct 1763 TB to Md Apr 1764. G.
- Gorbe, William. S Summer 1733 R Feb T Apr 1734 *Patapsco*. Sy.
- Gorman, Thomas. R 14 yrs Mar 1762 but pardoned same month for Army service. Ha.
- Gosling, Thomas. S Feb TB *New Trial* but removed from ship & pardoned Apr 1770. M.
Gosmore, John. S Summer 1741 R 14 yrs Feb 1742. So.
- Gold, John. S Lent R Jly T Sep 1730 *Smith*. E.
- Gold, Thomas. S Summer 1740 R 14 yrs Feb 1741. Ha.
Gough, Elizabeth wife of William, soldier. S Bristol May 1735. G.
- Goulding, Charles. S May but R for Navy Aug 1761. M.

- Goulstone, Mary. R & T 14 yrs Jan 1722 *Gilbert* LC Annapolis Jly 1722. M.
- Govey, George. R Jun TB 14 yrs *Phoenix* . Ht.
- Gower, Thomas. R Jun T 14 yrs Sep 1766 *Justitia*. Ht.
- Grace, John. S Lent R 14 yrs Jly 1724. So.

Graham, John. S Bristol Jun AT Aug 1749. G.
- Graham, Martha of Lambeth, spinster. SQS Jan but pardoned Mar 1765. Sy.

Grammont, Francis. S Summer 1741 R 14 yrs Feb 1742, found at large Apr 1742. Bu.
- Grange, Eunice. S Mar R Jun T 14 yrs Dec 1758 *The Brothers*. Ht.
- Grainger, James. S Lent R Jly T Dec 1736 *Dorsetshire*. Sy.
- Granger, Richard. R 14 yrs Sep 1768 TB to Va 1768. De.

Grant, Judith. SQS Hull Easter 1745. Y.
- Grant, Simon. S Bristol Apr 1767 R 14 yrs & TB to Md Sep 1768. G.

Grant, Thomas of Wisbech. R Jly 1762. Ca.

Grar, Solomon. S Mar 1727 T *Expedition* from Bristol to South Carolina. Wi.
- Gravel, John. S Summer 1728 R 14 yrs Feb 1731. Wi.

Graves, Ann. SQS Hull Easter 1748. Y.
- Graves, James. R Feb T 14 yrs Jun 1764 *Dolphin*. K.
- Gray, Anne of Woolaston. R for America Feb 1713 & Jun 1714. No.
- Graydon, Christopher. S Summer 1737 R Feb T 14 yrs Jun 1738 *Forward*. E.
- Green, Benjamin. S Lent but pardoned Apr 1768. Wa.
- Green, Charles. S Summer 1740 R Feb T 14 yrs Apr 1741 *Speedwell* or *Mediterranean*. Sy.
- Green, Edward. R Jun T 14 yrs Sep 1766 *Justitia*. K.
- Green, Elizabeth. S for murdering her bastard child Mar R 14 yrs Jly 1725. So.

Green, Francis. R for life Mar 1769. Be.
- Green, George. S Lent R Jun T 14 yrs Oct 1738 *Genoa*. Sy.
- Green, James. R Aug 1738 T 14 yrs Apr 1739 *Forward*. E.
- Green, Joseph. S Aug 1757 R Feb T 14 yrs Sep 1758 *Tryal*. Sy.
- Green, Joseph. R Jun T 14 yrs Sep 1766 *Justitia*. Sy.
- Green, Richard. S Bristol May 1763 R 14 yrs & TB to Md Apr 1764. G.

Green, Sarah. SQS Bristol & TB to Md Apr 1764. G.
- Green, Thomas. S Mar R Jun T 14 yrs Dec 1758 *The Brothers*. E.
- Green, Thomas. S Jan TB *Dolphin* but R for Navy Feb 1762. L.

Green, Timothy of Holbeach. R for America Feb 1718. Li.
- Green, Walker. R Sep T 14 yrs Oct 1722 *Forward* LC Annapolis Jun 1723. L.

Greenhill, John. R for Barbados May 1664. L.

Greening, Robert. S Bristol Mar 1741. G.
Greenslade, John (1753). *See* Webber, William. De.
* Greenslade, William. R 14 yrs Sep 1768 TB to Va 1768. De.
* Greenwell, Acton of Bermondsey. SQS Jan TB *New Trial* but pardoned Feb 1770. Sy.
* Greeve, Elizabeth wife of John. S Oct 1768 TB *Thornton* but pardoned Jan 1769. M.
* Gregory, John. S s horse Lent R & T 14 yrs Oct 1758 *Lux* from London. Db.
* Griffin [*not Griffith*], Henry. S Summer 1742 R Feb T 14 yrs Apr 1743 *Justitia*. E.
Griffith, Elizabeth, wife of John. S Oct 1733 & to be delivered to William Jefferis, merchant. G.
Griffith, Frances. R 14 yrs Bristol Apr 1742. G.
* Griffith, William. S Lent R Jly T Sep 1730 *Smith*. E.
Griffiths, James. SQS Bristol Dec 1762 TB to Md May 1763. G.
* Griffiths, James. S Jan-Feb but R to T himself Mar 1774. M.
Griffiths, James Butler. R Oct 1730. LM.
Griffiths, John. S (Bristol) Mar 1722. G.
* Griffiths, John. SQS Apr 1773; was to have pleaded pardon in May 1773 but his ship had already left. M.
Griffiths, Mary wife of Griffith. S Bristol Jan 1750. G.
Griffiths, Paul. S Bristol Mar 1753. G.
Griffiths, Philip. S Bristol May TB to Md Aug 1769. G.
* Griffiths, Thomas of St. Olave, Southwark. SQS 14 yrs for receiving lead Jan 1769 TB *Douglas* but pardoned same month. Sy.
* Grigg, Richard. S Summer 1746 R 14 yrs Feb 1747. De.
* Grimes [*not Grimer*], George. S Lent 1762 R for life Apr 1763. Wa.
* Grindall, Joseph. S Jly 1775 but taken from ship & pardoned same month. L.
* Grimwood, Thomas. R May T 14 yrs Sep 1767 *Justitia*. E.
* Grindall, Joseph. S Jly 1775 but taken from ship & pardoned same month. L.
* Grommett, Francis. S Summer 1741 R Feb T 14 yrs Apr 1742 *Bond*. Bu.
Groves, Mary, spinster. S Bristol Aug 1737. G.
* Groves, Sarah wife of John. S Apr 1773 but pardoned same month. M.
Groves, William. S Bristol Mar AT Sep 1740. G.
Gudgeon, Susannah wife of John. S Bristol Jly AT Aug 1753. G.
* Gulley, Richard. R Jan-Feb TB 14 yrs *Thornton* but pardoned Mar 1772. M.
Gummerson, Richard. S Bristol Aug AT Sep 1742. G.
Gunner, Robert. S Bristol Aug 1753. G.
Gunter, Joseph of Wadhurst. R for Barbados or Jamaica Mar 1709. Sx.
* Gwillim, Lewis. S Apr TB *Tryal* but R to T himself May 1768. M.
Gwyn, Catharine. S Bristol & TB to Md Apr 1767. G.

Haddock, Ralph. S Summer 1746 R 14 yrs Jly 1747. Du.
- Hadley, Mary wife of John. S for receiving goods stolen at Halesowen by Shem Hadley *(qv)* Summer 1768; pardoned Jly 1769. Wo.
- Hagg, Paul. S Lent T Apr 1758 *Lux* from London. Db.
- Haggot, John. R 14 yrs Sep 1770 TB to Va. De.
- Haley, Richard. S Summer 1764; found at large in London Lent 1765 & on petition from Shresbury R 14 yrs Summer 1765. Sh.
- Halford, Ann wife of George. SQS Aug TB to Va but pardoned Nov 1762. Le.
- Hall, Arnold. S & TB Dec 1767 *Neptune* but taken from ship & pardoned same month. M.

Hall, Elizabeth. SQS Bristol Dec 1760 TB to Md Apr 1761. G.

Hall, George of Swanscombe. R for Barbados Jun 1671. K.
- Hall, Isaac. S Mar 1761 but pardoned for sea service same month. L.

Hall, John. S s horse Oct R Nov 1728. Ca.
- Hall, Joseph. R Feb 1730 T Mar 1731 *Patapsco* LC Annapolis Jun 1731. L.

Hall, Thomas of Northampton[shire]. R for America Feb 1696. No.

Hall, Thomas. S Bristol Jly AT Aug 1749. G.

Hall, Thomasine. R 14 yrs Dec 1764. De.

Hall, William. S Summer 1734 R 14 yrs Feb 1735. Ht.

Hall, William. SQS (Bury St. Edmunds) Jan 1774. Su.

Halsey, John (1714). *See* Carter. L.
- Ham, Henry. S Lent R 14 yrs Jly 1724. De.

Hamilton, John. S Bristol May 1740. G.
- Hamilton, Thomas. SQS Sep but R for Army service Oct 1761. M.

Hamilton, David of Exeter. R for America Jly 1696. De.

Hamilton, Thomas (1771). *See* Erskine. M.
- Hammack, Edward. S Oct TB Dec 1771 *Justitia* but pardoned same month. L.
- Hammond, John, a youth. R Aug 1737 T for life Jun 1738 *Forward*. Sy.

Hammond, Robert. S Lent R Jun 1727. Li.
- Hampton, Ester wife of William of Sawbridgworth & Great Hadham, yeoman. S Lent R Jly 1730 but delivered of a child, Sarah, in Hertford Gaol & T Dec 1731. Ht.

Hampton, Samuel. R 14 yrs Bristol Aug 1751. G.

Handman, James. R Jan 1722. LM.
- Hannah, James. S Summer 1741 R Feb T 14 yrs Apr 1742 *Bond*. Ht.

Hannam, Samuel. S Summer 1752 R Feb 1753. Ha.

Hannibus, Richard. S Jly 1758 R 14 yrs Feb 1759. De.

Harbour, Thomas. SQS Bristol Aug TB to Md Sep 1766 LC Annapolis from *Randolph* as Thomas Harborn Mar 1767. G.
- Harden, Elizabeth. S Apr-May but pardoned Jly 1775. M.
- Hardin, Joseph. S for smuggling tea & obstructing Customs Summer 1737; T respited for 6 months Oct 1738. Nf.

Harden, Susan, wife of William, woolcomber. S (Bury St. Edmunds) Mar 1772. Su.
Harding, John. S Lent R Jun 1727. Wa.
Harding, Joshua. R 14 yrs Bristol Mar 1737. G.
Harding, Mary. R 14 yrs Bristol Mar 1741. G.
Harding, Richard. S Summer 1761. Bu.
* Hardman, John. S Summer 1729 R Feb T Sep 1730 *Smith*. E.
Hardy, Philip. S Summer 1741 R 14 yrs Feb 1742. Nf.
Harksell, John. S for highway robbery Lent R 14 yrs Summer 1770. Bu.
Harman, Elizabeth, widow. S Bristol Aug 1743. G.
Harpur, Thomas. S Bristol Dec 1748. G.
Harrington, Elizabeth, spinster. R 14 yrs Bristol Sep 1749. G.
Harris, Benjamin. SQS Bristol Dec 1769 TB to Md May 1770. G.
Harris, Elizabeth, spinster. SQS Bristol Oct 1768 TB to Md Apr 1769. G.
Harris *alias* Haste, John. S Bristol Jly 1733. G.
Harris, John, mariner. S Bristol Feb 1735. G.
Harris, John. S 14 yrs Bristol for receiving May TB to Md Aug 1769. G.
Harris, Robert. S Bristol Dec 1750. G.
Harris, Susannah, widow. S Bristol Feb AT Mar 1738. G.
* Harris, William. S Dec 1768, case reviewed unfavourably, T Jan 1769 *Thornton*. M.
Harrison, Ann wife of Richard of Hull, blacksmith. SQS Hull Epiphany TB Feb 1760. Y.
* Harrison, Nathaniel. S Aug 1757 R Feb T 14 yrs Sep 1758 *Tryal*. K.
Harrison, Samuel. SQS Jly 1775. Su.
* Harrison *alias* Procter, William of St. Clement Danes. R for Barbados May 1664. M.
Harropp, George of Newcastle upon Tyne. R for America or Africa Jly 1705. Nl.
* Hart, Edward. S for highway robbery & R for life Lent 1770. Ca.
Hartland, William. S Bristol Feb 1741. G.
* Hartle [*not Hartley*], Thomas of St. Margaret Westminster. R Aug AT Oct 1701. M.
Hartley, John. R for Barbados, Africa or America Feb 1696. Y.
Harvey, Edward of St. Mary Magdalen, Taunton. R for Barbados Feb 1671. So.
Harvey, John. R Jun 1768. Do.
Harvey *alias* Newman, John. R 14 yrs Apr 1769. So.
Harvey, William, porter. S Bristol Mar 1742. G.
Harwood, Lydia of Lincoln[shire], widow. R for America Feb 1696. Li.
Hasket, Joseph. R for s salt from warehouse Jun 1736. Ha.
Haslewood, John of Swanscombe. R for Barbados Jun 1671. K.
Haste, John (1733). See Harris. G.

- Hatch *alias* Deeble *alias* Dinham, Joseph. S Lent R 14 yrs Jun 1746. De.
- Hatch, William. S Dec 1772 but pardoned Feb 1773. M.
- Hatcher, George. S Lent R Jly T Dec 1734 *Caesar*. K.
- Havilock, John. S May-Jly but pardoned Aug 1773. M.

Haward, Robert. SQS Hull Mar 1760. Y.
- Hawes, Thomas. S Sep-Oct TB *Justitia* but pardoned Nov 1771. M.

Hawkins, Thomas. S Bristol Sep 1735. G.
- Hawkins, William. S Feb but pardoned Apr 1775. L.

Hay, Marjery wife of Col. John. R for life for high treason Jan 1725. LM.

Hayes, Darby, mariner. S Bristol Feb AT Mar 1742. G.

Hayes, John of St. Stephen's. S Bristol Mar 1752. G.
- Haylock, Abraham. S Lent R Jly T Dec 1734 *Caesar*. E.
- Haynes, Henry. R May T 14 yrs Sep 1767 *Justitia*. Sx.
- Haines, Isaiah. S s lead from Lady Beauclerk at Somerset House Jan TB *Tryal* but pardoned Feb 1764. M.

Haynes, Jacob. S Lent R May 1733. De.
- Haines, John. S & TB Apr 1766 *Ann* but R to T himself Sep 1766. L.

Haynes, Joseph. S Bristol Mar 1727. G.

Haywood, Ann. S for shoplifting Lent R Jun 1727. Wa.

Hazard, William. SQS Oct 1775. Nt.

Hazledine, Thomas. SQS Bristol Sep 1765 TB to Md Apr 1766. G.
- Head, Edward. S Lent R Jly T 14 yrs Sep 1742 *Forward*. Ht.
- Head, James. S May 1761 but pardoned same month. M.

Head, Mary (1722). *See* Bostock.

Heager, Lewis. R for Barbados or Jamaica Mar 1688. L.
- Healey, John. S Jun TB Jly 1772 *Tayloe* but pardoned same month. L.

Heath, Philip. R to T himself 7 yrs Nov 1775. L or M.
- Heath, Robert. R Jun T 14 yrs Sep 1766 *Justitia*. K.
- Hedges, William. S Feb TB Apr 1769 *Tryal* but taken from ship & pardoned same month. M.

Hemings, Thomas. S Bristol Aug 1738. G.
- Henley, William. S Oct, case reviewed unfavourably, T Dec 1770 *Justitia*. M.

Hennah, William. S Bristol Aug 1737. G.

Henry, Charlotta, spinster. SQS Bristol Mar TB to Va May 1775. G.

Henry, John (1773). *See* Godfrey. Do.

Henry, Leonard. R Jan 1722. LM.

Hensey, Dr. Florence. To T himself for life for supporting French King Jun 1759. L.
- Henshaw, John. S Oct TB *Tryal* but pardoned Nov 1765. L.
- Henson, John. S Aug 1770 but pardoned same month. Le.
- Herbert, Benjamin. S Feb 1772 TB *Thornton* but pardoned same month. L.
- Herbert, William. R Apr but pardoned May 1773. M.

- Herbert, William. R 14 yrs for shooting at a patrol Jly 1775. M.
Herring, George. S Lent R 14 yrs Jun 1754. So.
Hesler, William. R 14 yrs Jun 1761. E.
- Hessey, Richard. S Feb R 14 yrs Jly 1758. Ha.
- Hetherington, Robert. SQS s saddle Oct 1755 but pardoned Jan 1756. Du.
- Hewitt, Thomas. S Apr TB *Phoenix* but pardoned for Navy service Jly 1759. M.
Hewling, Ann (1771). *See* Smith. G.
Hewson, David of St. Andrew Holborn. R for Barbados Jun 1671. M.
- Hibberd *alias* Hubbard, William. S Jan-Feb but taken from ship & pardoned Apr 1774. M.
Hickes, Thomas. R (Bristol) 14 yrs Sep 1750. G.
Hickey, David. R 14 yrs Sep 1768. Ha.
Hickman, Hannah, singlewoman. S Bristol Aug AT Sep 1742. G.
Hickman, William. R 14 yrs Feb 1736. K.
Hicks, John (1761). *See* Jones. G.
Hicks, John. SQS Bristol Mar TB to Va Apr 1773. G.
Hicks, Thomas. R 14 yrs Bristol Aug 1751. G.
Higgs, John. SQS Jly 1770 as incorrigible rogue. Sh.
- Higgs, Mary. S Summer 1741 R Feb T 14 yrs Jun 1742 *Bladon*. Sx.
- Higgs, William. SW Jly TB *Douglas* but pardoned same month. M.
- Higton, Paul. S Summer case reviewed unfavourably Aug 1768. Nt.
Hill, Elizabeth. SQS Bristol Sep 1762 TB to Md May 1763. G.
- Hill, James. S City Summer 1751 R 14 yrs May 1752. Y.
- Hill, John. R 14 yrs Aug 1760 but pardoned for Army service same month. So.
- Hill, John of St. Martin in Fields. SW Jun but pardoned Jly 1774. M.
Hill, Mathew. S Bristol Feb 1751. G.
Hill, Sarah. S Summer 1737 R 14 yrs Feb 1738. E.
Hill, Sarah, singlewoman. S Bristol Jun 1746. G.
- Hill, Susanna. S Aug 1772 R for life Mar 1773; then found at large & to be hanged. De.
Hillam, Thomas. SQ (Peterborough) & R to be T for life Apr 1773. No.
- Hillier, John. R 14 yrs Sep TB to Va Oct 1768. Wi.
Hillier, Mary. S Jly 1728 T *Expedition* from Bristol to South Carolina. G.
- Hills, Matthew. T Apr 1765 *Ann*, found at large & R Jun T for life Sep 1766 *Justitia*. K.
- Hinckley, Francis of Flamstead. R Aug 1718 & Feb 1719 T May *Margaret* LC Md Aug 1719; sold to William Black. Ht.
- Hipsley, George. S Summer 1730 R 14 yrs Feb 1731. So.
Hipseley, William, *alias* Quillick, Jeremiah. S Summer 1741 R 14 yrs Feb 1742. So.
Hiscox, Hester, spinster. SQS Bristol Dec 1770 TB to Va Mar 1771. G.
Hitchin, John. R 14 yrs Apr 1769. La.

- Hitchings, Richard. S Oct 1761 but R for Navy service same month. L.
Hoare, Sarah, widow. R 14 yrs Bristol Aug 1753. G.
- Hoar, Thomas. S Oct TB *Justitia* but pardoned to serve at sea same month. Sy.
- Hoardley [*not Hoadley*], Thomas. R Jun 1737 T Jan 1738 *Dorsetshire*. K.
Hobbs, John. S Bristol Sep 1735. G.
- Hobbs, William. S Lent R 14 yrs Jun 1746. So.
- Hobbs, William. R May T 14 yrs Sep 1767 *Justitia*. E.
- Hockaday, George. S Lent R 14 yrs Jly 1724. De.
- Hockaday, William. S Lent R May 1731 TB to Va. De.
- Hocking, Catherine. R 14 yrs for murdering her bastard child Jly 1724. Co.
Hodges, James. R 14 yrs Jly 1767. Ht.
Hodges, John. R for life Feb 1767. G.
Hodges, Samuel. R 14 yrs Apr 1769. So.
- Hodgson, John of St. Marylebone. S Feb R Jun T 14 yrs Sep 1764 *Justitia*; pardoned Jly 1768 while exiled in New York. M.
Hodson, Norris. S Summer 1739 R Feb 1740. Sy.
- Hoffein, Goddard. S 14 yrs Sep-Oct but taken from ship & pardoned Nov 1773. M.
- Hoffman, Mary wife of John. S Apr-May but taken from ship & pardoned Jly 1775. M.
Holbrook, Ann. SQS Summer 1768. Sh.
Holden, Richard. R Mar 1725. Ht.
Holden, Thomas. SL & T Oct 1754 *Ruby*. Sy.
Holder, Edward. S. Bristol Sep 1730. G.
Holl, Elizabeth. R 14 yrs Apr 1771. He.
Holland, Ann (1704). *See* Denton. M.
- Holland, John. S Jly but pardoned Sep 1774. Ha.
Hollard, John (1696). *See* Markes. So.
Hollandsby, Stephen. R 14 yrs Feb 1764. Ha.
- Hollis, William, *alias* Berk, Thomas. SQS Dec 1772 but taken from ship & pardoned Mar 1773. M.
Holloway, William (1714). *See* Johnson. M.
Holman, Nicholas of Sandwich. R for Barbados Jun 1671. K.
Holmes, George. S Lent R Jly 1724. De.
- Holmes, John. R Jun 1737 T Jan 1738 *Dorsetshire*. Sy.
- Holmes, John. S s flour at St. Helen's Summer but pardoned Aug 1757. Be.
Holmes, Thomas of York Castle. R for Africa or America Jly 1715. Y.
- Holyoake, David [*not Daniel*]. S s sheep Lent R 14 yrs Summer & respited Sep 1767. Wa.
Hood, Robert. S Summer 1748 R May 1749. Nl.
Hooper, Edward. R 14 yrs Apr 1769. Ha.

- Hooper, John of Cleeve. R for parts overseas Jly 1719. G.
- Hooper, John. S Lent R Jly 1726. Do.
Hooper, John. S Mar R Jly 1728. Do.
Hooper, John. S Bristol Aug 1729. G.
Hooper, William. R 14 yrs May 1768. Wo.
Hopkins, Elizabeth, singlewoman. S Bristol Mar 1740. G.
Hopkins, Jane, singlewoman. S Bristol Feb 1739. G.
Hopkins, William of Fremington. R for America Jly 1696. De.
Hopkins, Zachariah. SQS Bristol Sep 1764 TB to Md Apr 1765. G.
Horler, John. SQS Bristol Dec 1771 TB to Va Feb 1772. G.
Horne, George of Lincoln[shire]. R for America Feb 1696. Li.
Horner, John. R 14 yrs Jun 1766. Sy.
Horner, Thomas. R 21 yrs Apr 1770. Ht.
Horton, John (1760). *See* Bowers, Thomas. Wo.
- Houching, Susan. S Summer 1740 for murder R Feb T 14 yrs Apr 1741 *Speedwell* or *Mediterranean*. E.
Houlton, Anne. S Bristol Jan AT Feb 1743. G.
Houlton, Habbacuck. SQS Bristol Mar TB to Md May 1763. G.
Houndsworth, Alice, spinster. S Bristol Nov 1735. G.
Housley, John. S Summer 1727 R Jly 1728. Wa.
How, John. R Mar 1725. Ht.
How, John. SQS Bristol Apr TB to Md May 1770. G.
How, Robert. S Bristol Aug 1736. G.
Howard, Alice, spinster, *alias* wife of John of Wandsworth. R for Barbados Jun 1671. Sy.
- Howard, James. SL Jly 1761 but R to serve in 49th Regiment in Jamaca same month. Sy.
Howell, Samuel. S Bristol Feb 1733. G.
Howell, Sarah, singlewoman. S Bristol Aug AT Sep 1741. G.
- Hownsome, William. R Apr T 14 yrs Apr 1770 *New Trial*. Sy.
- Howsden *alias* Newstead, Jane of St. Andrew Holborn, spinster. R for America May 1704. M.
Hubbard, William (1774). *See* Hibberd. M.
Huddin, James of Walsall. R for parts overseas Jly 1719. St.
Hudson, Ann. SQS Hull Epiphany 1746. Y.
Hudspeth, William (1769). *See* Todd. Nl.
Huggins, Thomas. R 14 yrs Mar 1773. Be.
- Hughes, Deborah. S Jly 1760, taken aboard *Phoenix* but removed to Newgate & shipped later in 1760. M.
Hughes, John. S Bristol Mar 1742. G.
- Hughes, Michael. SW Jly but pardoned Aug 1773. M.
Hughes, Thomas, mariner. S Bristol Aug 1739. G.
Hughes, William. S Bristol Sep 1731. G.
- Hughes, William Sr. S for murder Summer 1747 R 14 yrs Jan 1748. So.
Hume, Denison. SQS Bristol & TB to Md Sep 1770. G.

- Humphries, Charles. S 14 yrs for receiving Lent but pardoned Apr 1768. Wa.
- Hundy, Thomas. S s at St. Martin, Worcester, Lent but pardoned Mar 1774. Wo.
- Hunt, James. S Jly 1758 R Feb T 14 yrs Apr 1759 *Thetis*. E.
- Hunt, Robert. S lent T 14 yrs Jly 1764 *Justitia*. Ht.

Hunt, Simon. SQS Bristol Aug TB to Md Sep 1763. G.

Hunt, Thomas. R (Western Circuit) for America Jly 1696. L.

Hunt, Thomas, saddler. R 14 yrs Bristol Aug 1751. G.

- Hunt, William. R Jun T 14 yrs Dec 1758 *The Brothers*. K.

Hunt, William. S Bristol Apr 1767 R 14 yrs & TB to Md Sep 1768. G.

Hunt *alias* Symonds, William. R 14 yrs Apr 1771. He.

- Hunter, Joseph. S Feb but R to serve at sea Mar 1761. M.

Hupton, John. S Lent R Jun 1723. Bu.

- Hurdley, John. R Jan-Feb TB 14 yrs *Thornton* but pardoned Mar 1772. M.

Hurne, William. S Bristol & TB to Md Apr 1767. G.

- Hurst, James. S Lent R Jly T Sep 1764 *Justitia*. K.
- Hurst, Sarah. S & TB Jly *Scarsdale* but pardoned Aug 1771. L.

Hussey, Thomas, brickmaker. S Bristol Jan 1739. G.

- Hutchens, Mary. S Summer 1741 R 14 yrs Feb 1742. De.
- Hutchens, Samuel. S Summer 1741 R 14 yrs Feb 1742. De.

Hutchinson, Richard. S Bristol Mar TB to Md Apr 1765. G.

Hutton, Charles, *alias* Read, Benjamin. S Lent R 14 yrs Jun 1746. Wi.

Hutton, Thomas. SQS Oxford & R 14 yrs May 1767. O.

- Hyam, George. S Summer 1740 R Feb T 14 yrs Apr 1741 *Speedwell* or *Mediterranean*. Ht.

Hynam, Martha. S Bristol Sep 1748. G.

Ilsen, William (1762). *See* Incell. L.
- Ingman [*not Ingram*], Grace. S Lent R Jun T Sep 1747 *Forward* LC Rappahannock May 1728. Nt.
- Ingram, Richard. R Aug 1718 T May 1719 *Margaret* but died on passage. Ht.
- Incell *alias* Ilsen, William. S & TB Apr 1762 *Dolphin* but R for Army service in Jamaica. L.
- Ingram, Richard of Flamstead. R Aug 1718 & Feb 1719 T May 1719 *Margaret* but died on passage. Ht.

Inness, George, a young lad, native of Bengal. R to T himself for 7 yrs Oct 1766. L.

- Ireland, William. S Sep TB *Justitia* but pardoned Nov 1769. M.

Ireland, William. SQS Bristol Aug TB to Va Sep 1773. G.

Isles, Samuel. SQS Bristol Apr TB to Md May 1770. G.

- Israel, Moses. S as pickpocket Lent R 14 yrs but pardoned Apr 1766. Sh.
- Ivitt, Thomas of Wadhurst. R for Barbados or Jamaica Mar 1709. Sx.
- Izack, Samuel. S Feb TB *Dolphin* but R for Army service Mar 1762. M.

Jackson, Elizabeth, widow. R for Barbados May 1664. L.
Jackson, Elizabeth. SQS Bristol Oct 1765 TB to Md Apr 1766. G.
- Jackson, George. S Mar R Jun T 14 yrs Nov 1759 *Phoenix*. E.
- Jackson, John. S Bristol Apr 1767 R 14 yrs & TB to Md Sep 1768. G.
Jackson, Joseph of Morpeth. R for Barbados, Africa or America Feb 1696. Nl.
- Jackson, Mary. S Oct 1766 TB Jan 1767 *Tryal* but pardoned same month. L.
- Jackson, Mary. S Lent 1770 T by *Caesar* & shipwrecked, pardoned Dec 1770. Nl.
- Jacobs, Michael. S Mar R Jun T 14 yrs Dec 1758 *The Brothers*. E.
- James, George. S Oct 1761 TB *Dolphin* but R for Army service same month. M.
James, Henry. R 14 yrs Bristol Apr 1737. G.
James, Joseph. SQS Bristol Jly 1767 TB to Md Sep 1768. G.
- James *alias* Charles, Thomas of Llanthewy Skirrid. R for parts overseas Jly 1719; R Lent 1720 to T himself. Mo.
- James, William. S s at Magor Summer R for life Aug 1774. Mo.
- Jaques, George. S & TB Mar 1762 *Dolphin* but R for Army service same month. L.
Jaynes, James. SQS Bristol Jun TB to Md Sep 1767. G.
- Jeacocks [*not Jaycocks*], Thomas. R Jly TB 14 yrs Sep 1767 *Justitia* but R to T himself same month. M.
Jefferis, Hester, singlewoman. S Bristol Jly AT Aug 1741. G.
Jefferis, Margaret, singlewoman. S Bristol Jly AT Aug 1741. G.
Jefferis, Martha, spinster. S Bristol Jan 1737. G.
- Jefferson, John. S May-Jly but removed from ship & pardoned Jly 1774. M.
Jenkins, Charles. S Bristol Apr 1752. G.
Jenkins, Francis. R 14 yrs Bristol Oct 1740. G.
- Jenkins, Hannah. R Jun T 14 yrs Sep 1765 *Justitia*. Sy.
Jenkins *alias* Godwyn, Mary of Wells, spinster. R for Barbados Feb 1671. So.
Jenkins, Thomas. S Bristol Feb 1739. G.
Jenkins, William. S Bristol Feb 1750. G.
- Jenkins, William Glover of St. John's. SQS Oct TB Dec 1771 *The Brothers* but R for Navy same month. Sy.

Jennings, Anne, spinster. S Bristol May 1735. G.
Jennings, William. R 14 yrs Apr 1771. Be.
Jervis, Mary, spinster. S Bristol Aug 1737. G.
Jewitson, William of Molescroft. SQS Beverley Michaelmas 1754. Y.
Jiggle, William. R for buying stolen wheat & appeal rejected Dec 1750. Sy.
Jocham, John. S Bristol Mar 1753. G.
- Johns, Thomas of Godalming. SQS Jly TB Aug 1769 *Douglas* but pardoned same month. Sy.
Johnson, Benjamin. S Lent R Jun 1724. Db.
Johnson, Eliza. S Bristol Aug 1729. G.
Johnson, George, cordwainer. S Bristol Oct 1733. G.
Johnson *alias* Gonstan, George. SQS Hull Jun 1743 but escaped from gaol. Y.
Johnson, Gertrude, spinster. S Bristol Mar 1741. G.
- Johnson, Isaac. S Bristol Apr R 7 yrs & TB to Va Jly 1772. G.
Johnson, John. S Lent R Jly 1728. Li.
- Johnson, Joseph, aged 24, dark. S & T Oct 1720 *Gilbert* LC Annapolis May 1721; wife petitioned in Mar 1724 for his return. L.
- Johnson, Matthew. S Jun but pardoned Sep 1761. M.
Johnson, Moses. S Bristol Aug 1732. G.
- Johnson, Robert, *alias* Smith, William. S s gelding at Arncliffe & R 14 yrs Summer 1768 TB Apr 1769 but pardoned same month. Y.
Johnson *alias* Holloway, William of St. Pancras. R Jun 1714 & to remain in Newgate until transported. M.
Johnson, William (1771). *See* Smith, Henry. Sx.
- Jolle, John. S Lent R 14 yrs Jun 1734. De.
Jolliffe, Edward of Cranbourne. R for Barbados May 1664. Ha.
Jolly, William. S Mar 1728 R 14 yrs Feb 1729. O.
Jones, Anne, singlewoman. S Bristol Apr 1740. G.
Jones, Ann. R 14 yrs Bristol May 1743. G.
Jones, Ann, spinster. SQS Bristol Dec 1774 TB to Va May 1775. G.
- Jones, Charles. S Summer 1734 R Feb T 14 yrs Apr 1735 *Patapsco*. Ht.
Jones, Charles. SQS Bristol & TB May 1769 LC Rappahannock from *Brickdale* Aug 1769. G.
- Jones, Edward. S Lent T Jun 1756 *Lyon* but pardoned Jan 1758. Sy.
Jones, Eleanor of St. Giles in the Fields, spinster. R for Barbados Sep 1677. M.
Jones, Elizabeth wife of Charles. S Bristol Sep 1740. G.
- Jones, Evan. S s mare Lent R 14 yrs Mar 1767. Mo.
- Jones, Hannah of Coventry, spinster. R for America Feb 1713 & Jun 1714. Wa.
- Jones, Henry. S Nov TB Dec 1770 *Justitia* but R for sea service same month. L.

- Jones, Jane of Richmond, spinster. SQS Jan but pardoned Mar 1775. Sy.
Jones, Jeremiah. S 14 yrs Bristol for receiving May TB to Md Sep 1763. G.
- Jones, John. S Lent R Jly T Dec 1736 *Dorsetshire.* E.
Jones, John. S Bristol Nov 1747. G.
- Jones *alias* Smith, John. S Summer 1759 TB Mar 1760; found at large in Manchester & R for Army service Dec 1761. Db.
Jones *alias* Hicks *alias* Lister, John. S Bristol May 1761. G.
- Jones, John. S Jan but R for Army service Jly 1761. M.
Jones, John. SQS Bristol Sep 1769 TB to Md May 1770. G.
Jones, John. SQS Jan 1775. Sh.
Jones, Mary, spinster. S Bristol Mar 1741. G.
Jones, Mary, spinster. S Bristol Sep 1740. G.
Jones, Mary. S 14 yrs Bristol & TB to Md Apr 1764. G.
Jones, Richard of Lambeth. R for Barbados or Jamaica Mar 1709. Sy.
Jones, Richard Morgan. S Bristol May TB to Md Aug 1769. G.
Jones, Robert. R to T himself for life for sodomy Sep 1772. L.
- Jones, Samuel. S Lent R Jun T Dec 1736 *Dorsetshire.* Sy.
Jones, Thomas. S Lent R Jun 1723. Nf.
- Jones, Thomas. R Feb T 14 yrs Jun 1764 *Dolphin.* Sy.
Jones, Thomas. SQS Bristol Dec 1767 TB to Md Apr 1768. G.
Jones, Thomas. S Bristol & TB to Va Apr 1773. G.
Jones, Thomas Morgan. S Bristol May TB to Md Aug 1769. G.
Jones, Welthian, widow. S 14 yrs Bristol Apr 1743. G.
Jones, William. S Bristol Aug 1727. G.
Jones, William. S Lent R Jly 1730. Sy.
Jordan, Jane, spinster. S Bristol Nov 1753. G.

Kates, Robert. S Bristol Sep 1728 T *Expedition* from Bristol to South Carolina. G.
Katesmark, James. S Bristol Feb 1753. G.
Kear *alias* Caear, Thomas. R 14 yrs Mar 1767. G.
Keate, John of Stoke St. Gregory, husbandman. R for Barbados Jly 1671. So.
Keate, John. S Aug 1748 for highway robbery R 14 yrs Jun 1749. Du.
- Keaton, Michael. S for enlisting British subjects for King of France R 14 yrs Feb T May 1751 *Tryal.* K.
Kedby, Sarah. S (Bristol) Jun 1722 AT Apr 1723. G.
Keech, William. S for highway robbery Lent R 14 yrs Summer 1767. Bd.
Keedwell, George. R 14 yrs Jun 1768. So.
Keeling, Joseph (1737). *See* Fleming. Ht.
- Kellick, John. SQS & TB Apr 1765 *Ann* but pardoned same month. M.

- Kelly, George. S Lent R 14 yrs Jun TB to Va Sep 1744. Wi.
- Kelly, James. S Oct but taken from ship & pardoned Nov 1773. L.

Kelsey, Elizabeth. R for life Apr 1774. Sy.
- Kelson, Ann, spinster. S Bristol Apr R 14 yrs & TB to Va Jly 1772. G.
- Kemp, Benjamin. R Jun 1737 T Jan 1738 *Dorsetshire*. E.
- Kemp, Cornelius. R Jun T 14 yrs Sep 1766 *Justitia*. Sx.
- Kennedy, Lawrence. R for life s horse Lent but R to T himself Mar 1775. Ch.
- Kennedy, Patrick. S Apr-May for murder T 14 yrs Jly 1771 *Scarsdale*. M.

Kent, Elizabeth, spinster. SQS Bristol Dec 1772 TB to Va Apr 1773. G.
- Key, Richard. S Summer 1739 R 14 yrs Feb 1740. Co.

Keymess, John. S Bristol Sep 1734. G.

Keys, Mathias. R Sep 1747. E.
- Keyte, James of Blockley. R for parts overseas Jly 1719. Wo.

Keyton, Thomas. SQS Bristol Aug 1767 TB to Md Sep 1768. G.
- Kidder, Ann. S Oct TB *Justitia* but pardoned Nov 1769. M.

Kidder, William of Bletchington. R for Barbados Jun 1671. Sx.

Kierton, Samuel. SQS Hull Easter 1749. Y.

Killard, William (1768). *See* Skillard. De.
- Killigrew, Cornelius. S Summer & pardoned Aug 1774. E.

King, Ambrose of Thurrock. R for Barbados or Jamaica Mar 1709. E.

King, Joseph. S Bristol Feb 1737. G.

King, Thomas of Lamberhurst. R for Barbados Jun 1671. K.
- King, Thomas. R 14 yrs & TB to Va Mar but R for Army service Jly 1761. Wi.

King, William. SQS Bristol Aug 1764 TB to Md Apr 1765. G.

Kingston, John. S Bristol Aug 1749. G.
- Kingked, Alexander. S Summer 1718 R 14 yrs Aug 1719. Nl.
- Kinner, Thomas. SQS Oct TB *Justitia* but pardoned Nov 1771. M.
- Kipling, Robert. S Apr but pardoned May 1773. L.
- Kirby, William. S s sheep Lent R 14 yrs Summer 1764; noted as disordered in mind & pardoned Apr 1765. Bd.

Kirkwood, James. S Bristol Mar 1742. G.
- Kitson, Mary. SW & TB Nov *Neptune* but pardoned same month. M.

Kitto, William. R 14 yrs Sep 1768. Ha.

Knapp, Richard. S Summer 1740 R 14 yrs Feb 1741. So.
- Knight, Benjamin. S Lent R Jly 1726. Do.

Knight, Thomas (1736). *See* Parker. E.
- Knight, Thomas. S s at Whitchurch Lent 1761 T *Atlas* from Bristol but pardoned to serve in Army Aug 1761. Sh.

Knipe, Samuel. R for America for coining Mar 1699. Ch.

Knowles, Benjamin. R for Barbados May 1664. L.

Knowles, James. R 14 yrs Bristol May 1743. G.

Knowles, Thomas. S Bristol May TB to Md Aug 1769. G.

Lacey, William. S Bristol Jan 1734. G.
- Laidler, Thomas. S s horse & R for life Aug 1767 T *Caesar* and shipwrecked; pardoned for sea service Dec 1770. Nl.

Lake, Samuel. S Bristol Apr 1739. G.

Lamb, Christopher. S Bristol Apr 1767 TB to Md Sep 1768. G.

Lamb, Edward. S Bristol Aug 1725 to T himself to Barbados. G.
- Lamb, James. R Feb T 14 yrs May 1736 *Patapsco*. K.
- Lamb, Thomas. S for robbery in barn Lent R 14 yrs Jly 1728 TB to Va Oct 1729. Le.

Lance, Mary, widow. S Bristol Jly AT Aug 1741. G.
- Lander, John. SWK Jan TB Apr 1765 *Ann* but taken from ship & pardoned same month. K.

Landovery *alias* Dovey, Walter Burne. S Bristol Aug TB to Md Sep 1759. G.

Lane, Margaret. S Lent 1760. Bu.

Lane, Mary. S Oct 1733 & to be delivered to William Jefferis, merchant. G.
- Lane *alias* Roberts, Sarah, widow. S s paper at St. Dunstan in West Oct TB *Thornton* but pardoned Dec 1768. L.

Lane, Thomas. S Bristol Aug 1743. G.
- Lang, James. S Summer 1733 R 14 yrs Jun 1734. De.

Langham, Francis of Great Saxham. R for Barbados Jan 1665. Su.
- Langham, Joseph. S & TB Sep 1765 *Justitia* but pardoned Mar 1766. L.

Langsden, Mary. S Lent R 14 yrs Jun 1752. Sy.
- Langston, Robert. S Jan TB *Dolphin* but R for Army service Feb 1762. M.

Langville, Robert. S Bristol May TB to Md Sep 1766 LC Annapolis from *Randolph* Mar 1767. G.

Lantrow, George. R Nov 1769. So.
- Laremore, Daniel. S Jan-Feb but taken from ship & pardoned Apr 1774. M.
- Larkin, Benjamin. S Lent R Jly T 14 yrs Sep 1742 *Forward*. E.
- Larner, Ann. S Apr but pardoned Jun 1774. L.

*• Lamb, Thomas. S for robbery in barn Lent R 14 yrs Jly 1728 TB to Va Oct 1729. Le.

Lance, Mary, widow. S Bristol Jly AT Aug 1741. G.
- Lander, John. SWK Jan TB Apr 1765 *Ann* but taken from ship & pardoned same month. K.

Landovery *alias* Dovey, Walter Burne. S Bristol Aug TB to Md Sep 1759. G.

Lane, Margaret. S Lent 1760. Bu.

Lane, Mary. S Oct 1733 & to be delivered to William Jefferis, merchant. G.
- Lane *alias* Roberts, Sarah, widow. S s paper at St. Dunstan in West Oct TB *Thornton* but pardoned Dec 1768. L.

* Entries Lamb through Larner on pp. 50-51 are repeated from entries near top of this page.

Lane, Thomas. S Bristol Aug 1743. G.
- Lang, James. S Summer 1733 R 14 yrs Jun 1734. De.

Langham, Francis of Great Saxham. R for Barbados Jan 1665. Su.
- Langham, Joseph. S & TB Sep 1765 *Justitia* but pardoned Mar 1766. L.

Langsden, Mary. S Lent R 14 yrs Jun 1752. Sy.
- Langston, Robert. S Jan TB *Dolphin* but R for Army service Feb 1762. M.

Langville, Robert. S Bristol May TB to Md Sep 1766 LC Annapolis from *Randolph* Mar 1767. G.

Lantrow, George. R Nov 1769. So.
- Laremore, Daniel. S Jan-Feb but taken from ship & pardoned Apr 1774. M.
- Larkin, Benjamin. S Lent R Jly T 14 yrs Sep 1742 *Forward*. E.
- Larner, Ann. S Apr but pardoned Jun 1774. L.
- Larose, John. S Feb TB *Thornton* but on appeal of Hyme Larose taken from ship & pardoned Mar 1772. L.

Lash, Abraham. R 14 yrs May 1739. LM.
- Lash, Joseph. S Lent R Jly T 14 yrs Sep 1764 *Justitia*. K.

Latouch, Mary (1701). See Dyer. M.
Latwood, Christopher of Rockbeare, husbandman. R for America Jly 1696. De.
Laud, William (1770). See Lord. No.
- Law, John. S Jun T Aug 1769 *Douglas*; found at large & pardoned Jan 1773. M.
- Law, Samuel. S & R 14 yrs Summer 1766 [*not 1760*]. Bd.
- Lawrence, George of Burton on Trent. R for parts overseas Jly 1719. St.
- Lawrence, Henry. S Lent but R for Army service May 1756. Bu.

Lawrence, Sarah, spinster. S Bristol Nov 1753. G.
Lawton, John. R Lent 1763. Ha.
- Lazell, John. S Summer but taken from ship & pardoned Nov 1773. E.

Leeke, Hugh. R 14 yrs Aug 1771. Ht.
- Leake, James. R Jan T Feb 1726 *Supply* LC Annapolis May 1726. K.
- Lean, Richard. S s horse Summer 1730 R 14 yrs May 1733. De.
- Leary, Cornelius. S Bristol Apr for highway robbery R 14 yrs & TB to Va May 1774. G.

Lediard, Sarah wife of John. SQS Bristol Dec 1774 TB to Va May 1775. G.
Lee, Duke (1767). See Lee, Elisha. K.
Lee, Elisha *alias* Duke *alias* John. R 14 yrs Feb 1767. K.
Lee, John. S Bristol Apr 1736. G.
Lee, John (1767). See Lee, Elisha. K.
- Leigh, Mathew. S Summer 1740 R 10 yrs Feb 1741. So.
- Lee, Sarah. R Feb T 14 yrs May 1767 *Thornton*. K.
- Lee, Thomas. R Feb for being a gypsy T 14 yrs Nov 1762 *Prince William*. K.

Lee, Thomas. SQS Hull & TB Dec 1765. Y.
- Lee *alias* Leeworthy, William. S May T Jly 1753 *Tryal*; committed Jun 1758 for returning before expiry of term but acquitted because brought to England for court martial; pardoned Jan 1759. M.

Leeworthy, William (1753). *See* Lee. M.

Legg, Henry. S Bristol Jun AT Sep 1742. G.

Legg, John. S (Bristol) Aug R Sep 1748. G.

Lemon, William of Dartmouth, blacksmith. R for America Jly 1696. De.
- Leonard, William. S Jan-Feb but taken from ship & pardoned Apr 1774. M.
- Leng [*not Long*], Catherine wife of William. S for forgery May 1737, found pregnant, R Apr T 14 yrs Jun 1738 *Forward*. L.
- Lennon [*not Lemon*] *alias* Fyson, Thomas. S Lent R 14 yrs Summer 1747. E.

Lester, Thomas. S Bristol Aug 1749. G.
- Leverett, James. S 14 yrs Sep-Oct but taken from ship & pardoned Nov 1773. M.
- Levingstone *alias* Featherstone, Elizabeth. S Lent R 14 yrs Jly 1724. Ha.
- Lewin, William. S Apr but R for Army in Jamaica May 1761. L.

Lewis, Anne. SQS (Bristol) Apr 1723. G.

Lewis, Betty of St. Peter's, spinster. S Bristol Dec 1752. G.

Lewis, Elizabeth. SQS Bristol & TB to Md Sep 1761. G.

Lewis, Gabriel. R (Chester Circuit) for Barbados Nov 1666. X.

Lewis, Jane. S Aug 1727 T *Expedition* from Bristol to South Carolina 1728. Wo.

Lewis, Jane. SQS Bristol Jly TB to Md Sep 1765. G.

Lewis, John (1757). *See* Bazer.

Lewis, John. SQS Bristol Feb TB to Md Apr 1765. G.
- Lewis, John. S Sep TB Oct *Justitia* but pardoned Dec 1768. M.

Lewis, John. SQS Bristol Aug 1771 TB to Va Feb 1772. G.

Lewis, Margaret, spinster. R 14 yrs Bristol Sep 1749. G.

Lewis, Stephen. S Bristol Sep 1726. G.
- Lewis *alias* Chilvers, Susan of Whitechapel, spinster. R for America May 1704. M.

Lewis, Thomas. S Bristol Feb 1741. G.

Lewis, Thomas. SQS Bristol & TB to Md Apr 1764. G.
- Lewis, William. S Summer 1737 for forging deed of gift R 14 yrs Feb 1740. So.

Lewis, William. S Bristol Sep 1745. G.
- Lewis, William. S May 1765 TB *Justitia* but pardoned same month. M.
- Lewton, Thomas. S Bristol Apr R 7 yrs & TB to Va Jly 1772. G.

Lewy, Thomas. S Bristol Sep 1725. G.
- Lightbourn, Joseph. R Aug 1738 T 14 yrs Apr 1739 *Forward*. E.

Lill, Thomas of Bucknall, Lincs. SQS Hull Easter TB Apr 1758. Y.

- Lilly, John of Rotherhithe. SQS Jan TB Apr 1762 *Neptune* but R same month for Army service in Jamaica. Sy.
- Lillyman, Robert. S s horse Lent R Jly T Dec 1731 *Forward*. E.

Lincoln, John of Apstead(?). R for Barbados Jun 1671. Ht.

Lisle, William SQS Summer 1774. G.

Lister, John (1761). *See* Jones. G.

Liveings *alias* Going, Richard. R 14 yrs Bristol Mar 1737. G.

Llewellin, Edward. S Bristol Mar 1751. G.

Llewellin, Frances. SQS Bristol Aug 1764 TB to Md Apr 1765. G.

- Llewellin, William. S s ox Lent R 14 yrs Summer but pardoned to serve in Army Aug 1760. Mo.
- Lloyd, Anne. S Summer 1719 R Summer 1720 but pardoned Jan 1722. Nl.
- Lloyd, Edward of Wolverhampton, yeoman. S s horse Lent 1717 R for America Jly 1717 & Lent 1720. St.
- Lloyd *alias* Maund, Nicholas. S s at Ribbesford & Kidderminster but R for Army service Aug 1761. Wo.

Lloyd, Thomas SQS Easter AT Aug 1772. St.

Lock, John. SQS Jun TB to Va Sep 1773. G.

- Lockeskegg, Thomas. R 14 yrs Jun 1765; found at large & T for life Sep 1766 *Justitia*. K.

Lockwood, William of Mewell(?). R Jly 1703. Nf.

Lockyer, Thomas. S Summer 1754 R 14 yrs Feb 1755. So.

Lockyer, William. S Bristol Apr 1749. G.

Lodowick, Lewis. S Bristol Dec 1749. G.

Long, James. S Lent R 14 yrs Jun 1744. K.

Long, Richard. S Bristol Mar 1753. G.

Long, Richard. S Lent R 14 yrs Jun 1754. So.

Long *alias* Longman, William. R for Barbados May 1664. L.

- Longford, Elizabeth, spinster. SQS Bristol Mar TB to Va Jun 1771. G.

Longman, William (1664). *See* Long. L.

- Lord, John. R May T 14 yrs Sep 1767 *Justitia*. E.
- Lord, Mary. R Feb T 14 yrs Jun 1764 *Dolphin*. Sy.
- Lord *alias* Laud, William. S s horse & R 14 yrs Summer but taken from ship & pardoned Sep 1770. No.
- Lovegrove, James. S Bristol Apr 1767 R 14 yrs & TB to Md Sep 1768. G.

Lovell, Mary, singlewoman. S Bristol Aug AT Sep 1741. G.

Lovelock, William of St. George Southwark. R for Barbados Aug 1662. Sy.

- Lovett, William. S Aug 1760 but R for Army service overseas Aug 1761. So.

Lowance, John. SL & T Jly 1773 *Tayloe*. Sy.

Lowe, Ann. SQS Bristol Mar TB to Md May 1763. G.

Lowe, John. SQS (Peterborough) Lent R Apr 1755. No.

- Lowe, Samuel. S Jan & pardoned Feb 1773. M.
Lucas, Onesiphorus. S Bristol Oct 1749. G.
- Lucas, Stephen. S Lent but taken from ship & pardoned Apr 1775. K.
Lucas, Thomas (1760). *See* Luckes. Cu. & Y.
- Lucas, Thomas. S s at Devereaux Summer but R for Army service Oct 1761. He.
- Luckes *alias* Lucas, Thomas. S s sheep Summer 1760 R 14 yrs Jun 1761 but R for Army service same month. Cu. & Y.
- Ludlow, Henry, aged 11. SQS Feb TB *Thornton* R Mar 1768 to serve at sea until aged 21. M.
Lum, Richard. S Lent R Jun 1724. Li.
Lusty, Andrew. SQS Lent 1772. G.
- Lynch, Daniel. R Nov 1769 TB to Va 1770. De.
- Lynch, Eleanor. TB May 1764 *Dolphin* but pardoned same month. M.

McCanne, John. S Bristol Dec 1750. G.
McCawley, Henry. SQS Bristol May TB to Md Sep 1766 LC Annapolis from *Randolph* Mar 1767. G.
Macoppy, Jane (1722). *See* Bean. M
McCormick, Hugh, tailor. S Bristol Dec 1735. G.
McDaniel, Hugh. R 14 yrs Bristol Apr 1742. G.
McDaniel, Michael. SQS Bristol Dec 1773 TB to Va May 1774.
- McDonald, John. S Summer 1760 R 14 yrs Lent but R for Army service Aug 1761. Wo.
McGee, Richard (1763). *See* Potter. L.
McGraw, William. S Bristol May TB to Md Sep 1766 but died on passage in *Randolph*. G.
- McGuines, Bernard. R for life Jly 1765 TB to Va 1766. De.
McHone, Mathew (1740). See Mahone. G.
McKenley, Anthony. SQS Bristol Dec 1769 TB to Md May 1770. G.
Mackenzie, Charles. SQS Newcastle Apr 1770, shipwrecked on way to America & R for sea service Feb 1771. Nl.
McLane *alias* McCleane, Mary. S Bristol Aug 1750 for smuggling crowbars into Bristol prison. G.
- McQuire, Bernard [*not* Barbara]. S Lent R Jly T Dec 1736 *Dorsetshire*. E.

- Maeks *alias* Davison, Phebe, aged 22, servant. SQS s clothing Michaelmas 1774 but given free pardon in 1777. Nl.
- Maer, Alexander. S May TB Jun 1764 *Dolphin* but pardoned same month. L.
Magill, Patrick. S Bristol Jan 1750. G.

Mahone *alias* McHone, Mathew, mariner. S Bristol Aug AT Sep 1740. G.
- Maidman, James. R Aug 1730 T Apr 1732 *Patapsco*. K.

Mainwaring, Henry. Found at large after S of T & report requested Apr 1742. St.
- Malcah, Abraham. S Nov TB Dec 1770 *Justitia* but R for sea service same month. L.

Malins, John. S Lent R Jly 1728. Wa.
- Mallett, Joseph. S Lent R 14 yrs Jun 1734. De.

Malone, John. SQS Bristol & TB to Md Apr 1764. G.

Manger, Thomas. R 14 yrs Feb 1767 s sheep. Wa.
- Mann, Richard. R Jun 1737 T Jan 1738 *Dorsetshire*. Sy.

Mannery, John. R for Barbados or Jamaica Jly 1715. Sx.
- Manning, Henry. R Jun 1768 TB to Va 1768. De.
- Manning, John. S Feb but R for sea service Mar 1761. M.
- Mantle, David. S Bristol Apr R 7 yrs & TB to Va Jly 1772. G.

March, Thomas of Higham. R for America Feb 1718. Le.
- Marchant, Joseph. S Jan-Feb TB *Thornton* but R for sea service to East Indies Mar 1771. M.

Marchant, Thomas (1734). *See* Martin. Sx.

Marchant, William. SQS Bristol & TB May 1769 LC Rappahannock from *Brickdale* Aug 1769. G.

Markes *alias* Hollard *alias* Peyce, John of Bishops Lydeard, husbandman. R for America Jly 1696. So.

Marks, John, weaver. S Bristol Jan 1741. G.

Markwick, John. R 14 yrs Jun 1766. Sx.

Marlow, Jacob. S Summer 1741 R 14 yrs Feb 1742. Sx.
- Marlow, Mary [*not John*]. S for firing wood stack Lent R 14 yrs Summer 1748. No.
- Marrian, Walter. R to T himself 7 yrs Apr 1775. Wa.
- Marsh, George. SQS Bristol Feb TB to Md Apr 1761. G.

Marsh, Mary, *alias* wife of John Waters. S Bristol Sep 1744 AT Apr 1745. G.
- Marsh, Richard. SWK Oct 1773 but pardoned same month. K.

Marshall, Richard. SQS Bristol Feb TB to Md May 1770. G.

Marshall, Sarah (1704). *See* Stevens. M.

Marshall, William. SQS Newcastle Apr 1770, shipwrecked on way to America & R for sea service Feb 1771. Nl.
- Martin, Andrew. S & TB Jan *Tryal* but pardoned Feb 1767. M.
- Martin, Elizabeth. S Lent R Jun T 14 yrs Oct 1738 *Genoa*. K.

Martin, Elizabeth. SQS Hull Epiphany 1748. Y.

Martin, George of Elverton. R for America Jly 1696. Ha.

Martin, John of Bamber(?), husbandman. R for Barbados Jan 1665. Do.

Martin, Mary, spinster. S Bristol Sep 1749. G.

- Martin, Matthew. S Feb TB Apr 1770 *New Trial* but pardoned same month. L.

Martin, Richard of Great Torrington, husbandman. R for America Jly 1696. De.

Martin *alias* Marchant, Thomas. S Summer 1734 R 14 yrs Feb 1735. Sx.

Martin, Thomas. S Bristol Apr AT Sep 1744. G.

Martyn, William (1724). *See* May. De.

Massey, Mary (1701). *See* Dyer. M.

Masterson, John. S Summer 1742 R 14 yrs Feb 1743. E.

Mathews, Charity. S Bristol Aug 1750. G.

Matthews, Edmund. S Lent 1742 R 14 yrs Jun 1744. Wi.

Mathews, Elizabeth. S Bristol Sep 1727. G.

Mathews, Elizabeth, spinster. S Bristol Nov 1750. G.

- Matthews, James. S Feb 1761 but R for sea service same month. L.
- Mathews, Thomas. S Jun but R for sea service Jly 1761. M.

Mathews *alias* Methers, William. S Bristol July AT Apr 1739. G.

Matthews, William. R 14 yrs Apr 1771. Wo.

Matthews, William SQS Summer 1775. G.

Maund, Nicholas (1761). *See* Lloyd. Wo.

Maxwell, Thomas (1771). *See* Erskine. M.

- May, Catherine wife of John. S for shoplifting Lent R 14 yrs May 1733. De.
- May, Thomas. S Jly & pardoned Sep 1774. Ha.

May, William of Wapping. R for Barbados or Jamaica Aug 1700. M.

- May *alias* Martyn, William. S Lent R 14 yrs Jly 1724. De.

Mayo, Mary, spinster. S Bristol Aug 1743. G.

- Mayo, Thomas. S for highway robbery & R Lent but pardoned for Army service Jun 1762. Bu.

Mayris, William. S Lent R 14 yrs Jun 1755. Wi.

- Mead, John of Orsett. SQS Apr TB *Thetis* but R to serve in Army or Navy Aug 1757. E.
- Meade, Thomas. S Jly 1765 R Feb T 14 yrs Apr 1766 *Ann*. E.
- Meal, Henry. S as pickpocket Lent R 14 yrs May 1733. So.

Mechelborne, Thomas. S Lent R 14 yrs & T Oct 1760. Bd.

- Medcalf, George. S Summer 1740 R Feb T 14 yrs Apr 1741 *Speedwell* or *Mediterranean*. Sy.
- Mepham, Richard [*not Joseph*]. S Lent R Jly T 14 yrs Sep 1742 *Forward*. Sx.
- Merchant, Stephen Sr. S 14 yrs May-Jly but pardoned Aug 1773. M.
- Merchant, Thomas. S Lent R Jly T 14 yrs Sep 1742 *Forward*. Sx.

Meredith *alias* Williams, Joan. S Bristol Apr 1739. G.

Meriddee, William. R 14 yrs Bristol Apr 1737. G.

Merrick, Joseph (1696). *See* Merris. Wi.

Merris *alias* Merrick, Joseph of Calne. R for America Jly 1696. Wi.

Merrit, James. S Lent R 14 yrs Jun 1753. So.

Methers, William (1738). See Mathews. G.
- Metter, Thomasin. S Lent R 14 yrs Jun 1744 TB to Va 1745. De.
- Mewres, Samuel. S Summer 1746 R 14 yrs Summer 1747. Nl.

Meyer, Thomas. S Feb R 14 yrs Jun 1758. De.

Micklewright, Elizabeth. SQS s shoes Jan 1770. Sh.
- Miles, Christian. S & R Oct TB 1763 *Neptune* but pardoned same month. K.

Miles, John, butcher. S Bristol Nov 1736. G.
- Miles, Thomas. S for assault with reaping hook Lent but pardoned Jly 1762. He.

Millen, John. S Summer 1764 R 14 yrs Feb 1765. K.
- Miller, John. S Dec 1766 TB Jan 1767 *Tryal* but pardoned Mar 1767. L.
- Miller, Joseph. S Mar R 14 yrs Aug 1760. So.
- Miller, Maximilian. R to T himself Apr 1771; found at large & T Apr 1772 *Thornton*. M.

Millest, Thomas. S Summer 1743 R 14 yrs Feb 1744. Sy.
- Mills, Abel. S Summer 1741 R 14 yrs Feb 1742. De.

Mills, Ann wife of John. S Bristol & TB to Va Apr 1773. G.
- Mills, Nicholas. S Lent R 14 yrs Jun 1744 TB to Va 1745. De.
- Mills, William of Cherry Burton, yeoman. SQS Beverley Easter 1760. Y.

Milner, Thomas. S Lent R Jly 1728. Li.

Milton, Cornelius. SQS Feb TB to Md Apr 1764. G.
- Mitchell, John. S Summer 1729 R Feb T Sep 1730 *Smith*. K.

Mitchell, John. S Lent R Jly 1747. Sy.

Mitchell, William. S Summer 1741 R 14 yrs Feb 1742. Nf.
- Moffett, Samuel. S Oct TB *Justitia* but pardoned Oct 1771. L.

Mogg, John. S Summer 1772. Wa.

Molesworth, Daniel (1748). *See* Mould. De.
- Moll, Francisco. S Jan TB *Dolphin* but R for Army Oct 1761. L.

Molloy, Thomas. S Summer 1764 R 14 yrs Jun 1765. K.
- Moneypenny, Hugh. S Jan TB *Dolphin* but R for Army Dec 1761. L.

Montouth, Mary, spinster. S Bristol May AT Aug 1753. G.

Moon, James. S Summer 1741 R 14 yrs Feb 1742. Nf.

Moon, Prinor, widow. S Bristol Sep 1740. G.

Moore, John of North Petherton, husbandman. R for Barbados Feb 1671. So.
- Moore, John. T *Expedition* from Bristol to South Carolina 1728. Wi.

More, Joseph (1737). *See* Morey. Sy.
- More, Richard. S Summer 1741 R Feb T Apr 1742 *Bond*. Sy.
- Moor, Susanna. S Apr 1719 but pardoned same month. M.

Moore, William. R 14 yrs Feb 1767. Sy.

Moreman, Daniel (1748). *See* Mould. De.
- Morfield, William. S Summer 1741 R Feb T 14 yrs Apr 1742 *Bond*. K.

57

- Morey *alias* More, Joseph. S Summer 1737 R Feb T 14 yrs Jun 1738 *Forward*. Sy.
- Morgan, David. R Jun to be transported but pardoned for Army service Oct 1761. M.

  Morgan, Elizabeth wife of John. SQS Bristol Oct 1770 TB to Va Mar 1771. G.

  Morgan, Jane. S Bristol & TB to Md Apr 1767. G.

  Morgan, John. SQS Bristol Apr TB to Va May 1774. G.

  Morgan, Joseph. S Bristol Jly AT Aug 1749. G.

  Morgan, Margaret. SQS Bristol Dec 1765 TB to Md Apr 1766. G.
- Morgan, Sarah wife of Francis. S Bristol Apr R 14 yrs & TB to Va May 1774. G.

  Morgan, Thomas. S Bristol Feb 1742 AT Mar. G.

  Morgans, Morgan. S 14 yrs Bristol & TB to Md Apr 1764. G.
- Morris *alias* Clansey, Elizabeth of St. James Westminster, spinster. R for Barbados or Jamaica Mar 1688. M.

  Morris, Elizabeth. SQS Bristol Aug TB to Md Oct 1762. G.
- Morris, Henry of Westbury. R for parts overseas Jly 1717. G.
- Morris, James of Camberwell. SQS Feb but pardoned Nov 1773. Sy.
- Morris, John. S s fowls at Stanton Lacy Lent but pardoned Mar 1774. Sh.

  Morris, Richard. R 14 yrs Apr 1769. So.

  Morris, Sarah, singlewoman. S Bristol Jun 1747. G.
- Morris, William. S Lent R Jun T 14 yrs Oct 1738 *Genoa*. Sy.

  Morris, William. S Bristol Sep 1742. G.

  Morrison, William of St. James's. S Bristol Nov 1752. G.

  Mortimer, Philip. R for life Jun 1768. Ha.

  Mosely, George. S Summer 1750 R Feb 1751. Ha.
- Moses, Joseph. S Jly but R for Army service Oct 1761. L.
- Moss, Robert. S Lent R Jly T 14 yrs Sep 1742 *Forward*. E.

  Motley, Charles. S Bristol Jan AT Feb 1743. G.
- Mould *alias* Molesworth *alias* Moreman, Daniel. S Mar R 14 yrs Jun 1748. De.
- Moulson, William. R Feb T Sep 1730 *Smith*. E.
- Mound [*not Maund*], Rebecca of Stepney, spinster, *alias* Rebecca Dickinson, widow. PT Oct 1700 R Aug 1701. M.

  Mountain, Arthur. S Bristol Nov 1737 R 14 yrs for returning Sep 1740. G.

  Mountjoy, Martha. SQS Bristol Mar TB to Md Apr 1766. G.

  Mourne, Hugh. S Bristol Oct 1725. G
- Mullens, Henry. S & TB to Va Mar but R for Army service Aug 1761. Wi.
- Mullens, John. R Feb T 14 yrs May 1736 *Patapsco*. E.
- Munt, Jane. S Oct R for life Dec 1774. M.

  Murphy, Daniel. S Bristol Mar 1751. G.

- Murphy, John. S Jly R Sep T 14 yrs Oct 1722 *Forward* LC Annapolis Jun 1723.

  Murry, Duncan. SQS Bristol Jly 1764 TB to Md Apr 1765. G.

  Murry, James. SQS Bristol & TB to Md May 1763. G.

  Murrey, Roger of Dunster. R for Barbados Jly 1671. So.

- Naish, William. S Lent 1730 R 14 yrs Feb 1731. Wi.

  Nalder, Thomas. R yrs Nov 1769. Ha.

  Nash, John. R 14 yrs Bristol Apr 1742. G.

  Nash, Thomas. R Jly 1724. Wo.

  Naylor, Eleanor of Beeford, spinster. SQS Beverley Summer 1771. Y.

  Naylor, Isabella wife of Joseph of Kelfield. SQS Beverley Summer 1771. Y.

  Naylor, James. R 14 yrs Apr 1769. La.

- Neal, Thomas. S Lent R 14 yrs Jun 1749. Ht.
- Neighbours, Joseph. S Bristol Mar 1765 R 14 yrs & TB to Md Sep 1766 LC Annapolis from *Randolph* Mar 1767. G.
- Nesbitt, James. S Lent R Jun T 14 yrs Aug 1752 *Tryal*. K.

  Nettle, John. S Summer 1726 R Jly 1727. So.

  New, William. SQS Bristol Feb TB to Philadelphia Mar 1771. G.
- Newberry, Robert. S Mar for rape R Jun T 14 yrs Nov 1759 *Phoenix*. Sy.

  Newel, Robert. S Lent R 14 yrs Jly 1747. Hu.

  Newey, Thomas of Kingston on Thames. R for Barbados Jun 1671. Sy.
- Newman, Edward. S Oct 1773 but pardoned same month. L.

  Newman, John (1769). *See* Harvey. So.
- Newman, Joseph. S Summer 1730 R 14 yrs Feb 1731. Wi.
- Newport, John. S Mar 1761 but R for sea service same month. L.
- Newson, John. S Feb T Apr 1770 *New Trial* removed from ship to T himself then pardoned for sea service Dec 1770. M.

  Newstead, Jane (1704). *See* Howsden. M.

  Newth, Thomas. SQS Lent 1773. G.
- Newton, John. S Lent R 14 yrs May 1733. So.
- Newton, Thomas of New Sleeford. R for America Feb 1713 & Jun 1714. Li.
- Newton, Thomas. S Summer 1769 R 14 yrs Lent 1770, case reviewed but sentence to stand. Nt.
- Nicholas [*not Nicholls*], Matthias. S Oct for highway robbery R for life Nov 1750. M.
- Nicholls, Jonathan. S May TB *Justitia* but pardoned Jly 1765. L.

  Nicholson, Isabella, singlewoman. S Bristol Sep 1746. G.
- Nixon, Robert. S Mar R Jun T 14 yrs Sep 1758 *Tryal*. Sy.

  Nobbs, Henry. R for life for riotous assembly in Norwich Feb 1767. Nf.

- Norbury, Elizabeth. S 14 yrs Jan-Feb but taken from ship & pardoned Apr 1774. M.

Norris, John. S Bristol Mar AT Sep 1740. G.
- Norris, Richard. S Summer 1764 R Feb T 14 yrs Apr 1765 *Ann.* Sy.
- Norris, Thomas. S Summer 1733 R Jun 1734. So.
- North, John. S Apr but pardoned Jun 1773. M.
- Norton, John. S Feb 1774 but pardoned same month. L.
- Nott, William Sr. S Jly 1758 R Feb T 14 yrs Apr 1759 *Thetis.* E.
- Nott, William Jr. S Jly 1758 R Feb T 14 yrs Apr 1759 *Thetis.* E.
- Nowell, James. S Lent R 14 yrs Jun 1744. So.

- Oakden, George. R s horse Lent but pardoned Apr 1772. Wa.

Oar, Ann. S Bristol Mar 1736, found pregnant & R 14 yrs Aug 1738. G.

Oates, Winifred. SQS Bristol Mar TB to Md Apr 1768. G.

O'Bryan, Cornelius. SQS Bristol Aug TB to Va Sep 1773. G.

Obrien, William. S Lent R 14 yrs Jly 1747. Hu.

Odam, John. S Summer 1740 R 14 yrs Feb 1741. O.
- Odele, Edward. S Lent R Jly T 14 yrs Sep 1764 *Justitia.* Sy.

Odell, Thomas. R for life for highway robbery Nov 1750. LM.

Ogden, Judith (1750). *See* Butler. M.
- Old, John. S Summer 1741 R 14 yrs Feb 1742. Do.
- Oliver, Thomas. T *Expedition* from Bristol to South Carolina 1728. Wo.

O'Neil, Henry. SQS Bristol Sep 1763 but died before T. G.
- Oney, Samuel. S Summer 1729 R Feb T Sep 1730 *Smith.* Ht.
- Orr *alias* Cunningham, William. S highway robbery & T 14 yrs Summer 1773; Sep 1776 T for life for returning. Nl.
- Orrox, Elizabeth. S & TB Sep 1764 *Justitia* but pardoned Feb 1765. L.
- Orton, William. S Summer 1742 R 14 yrs Feb 1744. So.
- Orum, Benjamin of South Kilworth. R for America Feb 1713 & Jun 1714. Le.
- Osburn, George. SQS Bristol Mar Mar TB to Va Jun 1771. G.

Osborne, James. R 14 yrs Bristol Mar 1741. G.

Osbourne, John. S Lent R 14 yrs Jly 1747. Su.
- Osborne, John. S Bristol Apr R for life & TB to Va Jly 1772. G.
- Osburn, William. SQS Bristol Mar Mar TB to Va Jun 1771. G.
- Osmond, Edward. S Summer 1746 R 14 yrs Feb 1747. De.

O'Sullivan, Bryan (1700). *See* Sullivan. M.

Otin, Anne, spinster. S Bristol Jan 1737. G.

Ottway, James. R 14 yrs Jun 1766. Sy.

Ovens, Daniel. S (Bristol) Feb 1722. G.

Ovens, James. S (Bristol) Feb 1722. G.
- Ovins, Gilbert. R Aug 1765 T for life Apr 1766 *Ann.* Sy.

Owen, Edward. S Bristol & TB to Md Apr 1767. G.
Owlett, William of Hull, bricklayer. SQS Hull Easter TB Apr 1758. Y.

Pack, Thomas. S Lent R Jun 1727. No.
Packer, Daniel. S Summer 1773. Bu.
Page, John of St. Margaret Westminster. R for Barbados Sep 1677. M.
- Page, Joshua. S Lent R Jly T 14 yrs Sep 1742 *Forward*. E.
Painter, Edward. S Lent R 14 yrs Jun 1755. Ha.
Pallister, John. R Jun 1714 & to remain in Newgate until transported. L.
Pankhurst, Thomas. R 14 yrs Jly 1760. K.
- Pantry, Robert. S Lent but R to serve in 49th Regiment in Jamaica Apr 1761. Sy.
Paris, John. S Bristol Sep 1742. G.
Parker, Gerrard. S (Bury St. Edmunds) Jan 1775. Su.
- Parker, Martha of St. Nicholas, Worcester, singlewoman. S for shoplifting & R for America Jly 1717. Wo.
- Parmer, Robert. S Summer 1733 R 14 yrs Jly 1734. Ha.
- Paris, John. S Jan 1762 TB *Dolphin* but R for Army service in Jamaica same month. L.
- Paris, Richard. S Summer 1733 for highway robbery R Feb T Apr 1734 *Patapsco*. K.
- Parish, John. S Lent R for life Apr 1766. Nf.
- Parker, Edward. S Lent R Jun T 14 yrs Oct 1738 *Genoa*. Sx.
Parker, Richard (1737). *See* Wall, John. Ht.
- Parker, Robert. S Oct TB Dec 1770 *Justitia* but R for sea service same month. M.
- Parker *alias* Knight, Thomas. S Lent R Jly T Dec 1736 *Dorsetshire*. E.
- Parker, Thomas. S Summer 1746 R 14 yrs Summer 1747. Y.
Parlour, Mary. SQS Bristol Feb TB to Md Apr 1760. G.
Parnell, Richard. S King's Bench but found at large & R 14 yrs Feb 1763. Nf.
Parnham, Henry. S Lent R Jun 1724. Li.
Parnham, Thomas. S for housebreaking Lent R 14 yrs Summer 1770. Bu.
Parr, William. SQS Bristol Mar TB to Md May 1763. G.
Parricke, Mathew (1696). *See* Patricke. Li.
- Parrott, John Jr. R Apr T 14 yrs Dec 1771 *Justitia*. Sy.
- Parrott, Thomas. S Summer 1759 R 14 yrs Lent 1760 but pardoned for Army service in Jamaica Jly 1762. Li.
Parry, John (1767). *See* Sparey. St.
Parry, Mary (1748). *See* Perry. G.
Parry, Mary, spinster. S Bristol Aug 1743. G.
Parry, Thomas. R 14 yrs Apr 1773. Wo.
Parsons, George. S Lent R Jly 1724. So.
Parsons, Henry. S Lent R Jly 1724. So.

Parsons, Jane, spinster. S Bristol Oct 1749. G.
Partridge, Thomas. S Bristol Mar TB to Md Apr 1765. G.
Pasmore, Mary. S Bristol Feb AT Apr 1745. G.
• Paston, James. S Apr but pardoned May 1763. L.
Patricke *alias* Parricke, Mathew of Lincoln[shire]. R for America Feb 1696. Li.
Patrick, William. R 14 yrs Bristol Apr 1737. G.
Pattin *alias* Perrin, Elizabeth. S Bristol Nov 1749. G.
Paul, John. S Bristol Feb 1751. G.
Payles, Edward. S s mare Lent R Jun 1723. Bu.
Payn, Edward. S Bristol Jly 1725. G.
• Payne, William. S Summer 1764 R Feb T 14 yrs Apr 1765 *Ann*. K.
Payton, Henry. S Bristol Dec 1764 TB to Md Apr 1765. G.
Payton, William. S Bristol Mar 1753. G.
Peake, Ann. SQS 14 yrs for receiving Jan 1774. Sh.
Peak, William. S Lent R Jun 1724. Li.
Pearce, Benjamin. S Bristol R 14 yrs & TB to Va Apr 1773. G.
• Pearce, Edward. R Apr T Dec 1771 *Justitia*. Sx.
• Pearse, Elizabeth. S & TB 14 yrs Apr *Thames* but pardoned May 1753. L.
• Pearce, John. S Oct but pardoned Nov 1772. L.
• Pearce, Robert. S Lent R 14 yrs Jly 1724. Wi.
• Pearce, Thomas. S Apr 1774 but removed from ship in poor health & pardoned same month. L.
• Pearson, John. S Summer 1746 R 14 yrs Summer 1747. We.
• Pearson, Joseph. S Jly 1765 R Feb T 14 yrs Apr 1766 *Ann*. E.
Pearson, Mary of Carnaby. S Beverley Christmas 1770. Y.
• Peate, William. S Summer 1726 R Jun TB to Va Sep 1727. Le.
Peeke, John (1760). *See* Cripps. So.
Peirce, Ann. SQS Bristol Sep 1763 TB to Md Apr 1764. G.
Pellamenter, Nicholas, mariner. S Bristol Feb 1739. G.
Pennyman, George. S Summer 1729 R Feb 1731. Wi.
Percy, Thomas Pinke (1772). *See* Pinke. G.
Perrin, Elizabeth (1749). *See* Pattin. G.
Perrott, John. S Bristol Sep 1742. G.
Perry, Dionysius. S Bristol Sep 1753. G.
Perry, Mary, widow. S Bristol Aug 1734. G.
Perry or Parry, Mary, singlewoman. S Bristol Mar AT Apr 1748. G.
Perry, Walter. S Bristol Nov 1734. G.
Peterson, John (1755). *See* Dayly. L.
Pewd, Thomas. S Jly 1759 R 14 yrs Feb 1760. Wi.
Peyce, John (1696). *See* Markes. So.
Phillips, Ann of Reading. R for parts overseas Jly 1719. Be.
Phillips, Anne. S 14 yrs Bristol Mar 1738. G.
Phillips, David (1768). *See* Thomas. G.

- Phillips, Evan. S Lent R 14 yrs Summer 1760 T 1761 *Atlas* from Bristol but pardoned for Army service Aug 1761. He.

Phillips, George. SQS Bristol Jun 1760 TB to Md Apr 1761. G.

Phillips, George. SQS Bristol Aug TB to Md Sep 1767. G.

Phillips, John. S Bristol Mar 1737. G.

Phillips, John. SQS Bristol Oct 1766 TB to Md Apr 1767. G.

- Phillips, Ralph. T *Expedition* from Bristol to South Carolina 1728. G.

Phillips, Sarah, spinster. S Bristol Aug 1749. G.

- Phillips, Thomas. S Bristol s ox May 1766 R 14 yrs & TB to Md Apr 1767. G.
- Phipps, Mary wife of Edward. S s sheep Lent R 14 yrs Mar 1767. Mo.
- Phipps, Stephen. S s horse Lent R 14 yrs May 1731. Ha.

Pickett, Henry. R to be T for life Mar 1773. Ht.

Pickford, Robert. S Summer 1741 R 14 yrs Feb 1742. Do.

Piercy, Peter. R for murder Aug 1726. L.

- Piggott, John. S Summer 1764 R Feb T 14 yrs Apr 1765 *Ann*. Ht.
- Piggott, Ralph. S Summer 1742 R Feb T 14 yrs Apr 1743 *Justitia*. Ht.

Pim, John, yeoman. S Bristol Sep 1740. G.

Pim, William. SQS Bristol Apr TB to Md May 1770. G.

Pinchbeck, Benjamin. S Lent R Jun 1724. Li.

- Pinke, Thomas, *alias* Percy, Thomas Pinke. S Bristol Apr R for life & TB to Va Jly 1772. G.
- Pinkstone, Thomas. R for life Feb 1775 & to T himself. M.
- Pitchey, George. S Jly 1757 R Feb T 14 yrs Sep 1758 *Tryal*. E.

Pitt, Henry of Laverstock. R for America Jly 1696. Wi.

Pitt, John SQS Lent 1775. G.

- Pitt, Richard. S Lent R 14 yrs Summer 1760 T 1761 *Atlas* from Bristol but pardoned for Army service Jly 1761. He.

Pitt, William. R for life Aug 1758. G.

Pitts, Martha. R 14 yrs Nov 1769. Ha.

- Plessis, Nicholas. S Jan TB *Dolphin* but R for Army service Feb 1762. M.
- Plumb, John. S Feb but taken from ship & pardoned Mar 1773. L.

Plumbe, John. R for life for highway robbery Apr 1775. K.

- Pollard, John. S 1761 but R to serve in 49th Regiment in Jamaica Apr 1761. K.

Pollard, Richard (1763). *See* Potter. L.

Pook, William. S Bristol Mar 1751. G.

Poole, Mary, singlewoman. S Bristol Sep 1744 AT Apr 1745. G.

Pool, Mary. SQS Lent 1770. Sh.

Poole, Richard. SQS Bristol Aug TB to Md Oct 1762. G.

Pope, Samuel. SQS Bristol Mar TB to Md Apr 1768. G.

- Popplewell, Joseph [*not John*]. S Sep-Oct but R to T himself Nov 1774. M.
- Porter, Jasper. S Lent R 14 yrs Jly 1724. Wi.

Porter, Jeremiah of St. Andrew Holborn. R Jun 1714 & to remain in Newgate until transported. M.
Porter, William of St. Saviour Southwark. R for Barbados Jun 1671. Sy.
* Porter, William. R 14 yrs Aug 1765. So.
* Potter *alias* Pollard *alias* McGee, Richard. R Aug T 14 yrs Dec 1763 *Neptune*. L.
* Powell, Anthony. TB Apr 1762 *Neptune* but R same month for Army service in Jamaica. Ht.
Powell, David. S Bristol Mar 1738. G.
Powell, Edward. SQS Bristol Sep 1766 TB to Md Apr 1767. G.
Powell, John. S Bristol Aug 1729. G.
* Powell, John. TB Apr 1762 *Neptune* but R same month for Army service in Jamaica. Sy.
* Powell, John. S Lent R 14 yrs Mar 1767. Mo.
Powell, William of St. Andrew Hertford. R for Barbados Jun 1671. Ht.
Powell, William. S Bristol 1764 R 14 yrs Mar TB to Md Apr 1765. G.
* Pownall, John. R Feb T Sep 1730 *Smith*. E.
Poxon, Thomas. S Lent R Jun 1727. Le.
* Pratt, Alexander, aged 23, husbandman. SQS s cloth Easter 1775 but in Morpeth Prison in Dec 1775. Nl.
Pratt, Mary, singlewoman. S Bristol Dec 1740. G.
Prattin, Robert. S Bristol Sep 1740. G.
* Prescott, Mary. TB Apr 1764 *Dolphin* but pardoned same month. E.
* Presly, John. S Lent R 14 yrs Jun 1746. Wi.
* Prestidge, John. S Summer 1739 R Feb T Jun 1740 *Essex*. Ht.
Price, Alisha, spinster. S Bristol Nov 1753. G,
Price, Henry. SWS (Bristol) Apr 1723. G.
Price, James. S Bristol Nov 1728. G.
Price, John. S Bristol Aug 1751. G.
Price, Lewis. S Bristol Feb 1751. G.
Price, Olive, widow. S Bristol Aug R 14 yrs Sep 1739. G.
Price, Richard. S Summer 1723 R Feb 1724. Mo.
Price, Susannah (1770). *See* Thomas. G.
Price, Thomas. S Sep R Nov 1726. De.
Price, Trephana, spinster. SQS Bristol May TB to Va Jly 1772. G.
* Price, William. R 14 yrs Nov 1750. M.
* Pricklow, John of Godalming. SQS Oct 1761 but R for Army service same month. Sy.
Priddy, Mary, spinster. S Bristol Feb 1736. G.
Pritchard, Mary. SQS Bristol Aug TB to Md Sep 1761. G.
Pritty, Elizabeth wife of James. S Bristol Feb 1753. G.
Probert, James. S Lent 1768. Bu.
Procter, William (1664). *See* Harrison. M.
Prosser, Richard. S Bristol May 1728. G.
Prosser, William. S Bristol Jan 1742. G.

Provis, William. R 14 yrs Jun 1768. Co.
Prowse, James of St. James's. S Bristol May 1752. G.
* Pugh, Arabella of Bristol. R Oct 1761 but pardoned same month. G.
Pugh, Isabella. SQS Bristol Sep 1760 TB to Md Apr 1761. G.
Pugh, John. SQS Jly 1770 as incorrigible rogue. Sh.
* Pugh, John William. S Jan-Feb but taken from ship & pardoned Apr 1774. M.
* Pullen, Charles. S Oct 1774 but pardoned same month. L.
* Pullen, John. R 14 yrs as pickpocket Jun 1736. So.
* Punter, Thomas. S Lent TB Apr 1755 but pardoned same month. G.
Purcell, Henry. S Lent R Jun 1730. Sy.
* Purdue, Thomas. S 14 yrs for receiving hens stolen by John Snow *(qv)* Lent but pardoned Mar 1766. Be.
Purnell, William. S Mar 1727 T *Expedition* from Bristol to South Carolina. Wi.
* Putnam, James. S Summer TB Sep *Justitia* but pardoned Nov 1764. Bu.
* Puttyford, John. S Dec 1761 TB *Dolphin* but R for Army service same month. M.
Pybus, John. SQS Hull Epiphany 1774. Y.
* Pyne, Charles. S Jan TB Apr 1770 *New Trial* but R same month to T himself. M.

Quaquo, Mary wife of Thomas, sailor. S Bristol May T Jun 1732. G.
Quillick, Jeremiah (1741). *See* Hipseley, William. So.
* Quynn, John. S Summer 1741 R Feb T 14 yrs Apr 1742 *Bond*. K.
* Quin, Thomas. S Oct 1761 TB *Dolphin* but R for Army service same month. M.
* Quincey, John. S Jly 1761 but pardoned same month. L.
* Quint, Andrew Jr. S Summer 1746 R 14 yrs Feb 1747. De.
Quinton, James. R 14 yrs Aug 1773. Nl.

Raby, Elizabeth. SQS Hull Epiphany 1749. Y.
* Rackley, Elizabeth. S Dec 1766 but pardoned Apr 1767. G.
* Radcliffe, Charles. S 14 yrs for receiving goods stolen at St. Chad by John Cope *(qv)* Lent but pardoned Apr 1766. St.
* Radcliffe, John. S s cloth from tenters Lent but pardoned Apr 1775 Y.
Radford, John. S Bristol Apr 1739. G.
Ragborne, Robert of Burbage, husbandman. R for Barbados Feb 1671. Wi.
* Rainbird *alias* Garland, Joseph. R Nov 1750 T for life May 1751 *Tryal*. K.
* Ralph, Thomas. S Lent but R to serve in 49th Regiment in Jamaica Apr 1761. K.

Ram, George. S Lent R Jly 1724. Ha.
- Randall, Thomas. S Mar but pardoned Apr 1773. Ha.
- Ranger, John [*not Job*]. S Lent 1742 R 14 yrs Jun TB to Va Sep 1744. Wi.

Ratcliffe, James. S Summer 1731 R Apr 1732. E.

Raymond, Andrew. R Sep 1722. LM.

Read, Alexander. S Bristol Mar 1736. G.

Reed, Ann. SQS Hull Epiphany 1756. Y.

Read, Benjamin (1746). *See* Hutton, Charles. Wi.

Reed, John. R Nov 1769. So.
- Reed, Martin. R Jun TB 14 yrs *Phoenix* but pardoned for Army service Sep 1759. Sy.
- Read, Sarah [*not Samuel*]. S Lent R Jly T Dec 1734 *Caesar*. E.

Read, William. R 14 yrs Sep 1768. Ha.
- Reading, Lambeth. SW & TB Oct 1769 *Justitia* but pardoned same month. M.

Reading, Thomas. S Bristol May 1728. G.
- Reddall, William. S Lent but pardoned Apr 1766. Wa.

Redhead, Thomas. R 14 yrs May 1750. L.

Redman, Sarah. SQS Bristol Aug TB to Md Sep 1763. G.

Redwood, Thomas, tobacco pipemaker. S Bristol Feb 1736. G.
- Redwood, William. S Dec 1772 but taken from ship & pardoned same month. M.

Reece, Catharine. SQS Bristol Feb TB to Md Apr 1765. G.

Reece, David of St. James's. S Bristol Sep 1752. G.

Reece, Thomas. S Bristol May TB to Md Sep 1766 LC Annapolis from *Randolph* Mar 1767. G.

Reeves, Margaret, wife of Peter. S Bristol Aug AT Sep 1740. G.

Regis, Vittorio. T Jly 1770 *Scarsdale* from Newgate. L or M.
- Renshaw, Isabella. S May TB Aug 1766 *Justitia* but pardoned same month. L.
- Revel, James. T Apr 1771 *Thornton*, taken from ship on appeal but sentence upheld. Sy.
- Revell, John. S Lent R Jly 1730 T Apr 1731 *Bennett*. E.
- Reynolds, Edward. S Feb TB Mar 1770 *New Trial* but R to T himself same month. L.
- Rhoads, James. S Bristol Apr R 14 yrs & TB to Va Jly 1772. G.

Rice, Samuel. S Bristol Aug 1729. G.
- Rice, Valentine. S Summer 1734 R 14 yrs Feb 1735. De.
- Rich, John. S Lent 1728 R 14 yrs Feb 1731. Wi.

Richards, Elizabeth, spinster. S Bristol Apr R 7 yrs & TB to Va Jly 1772. G.
- Richards, Frederick. S & TB Apr *Ann* but removed from ship & pardoned Aug 1766. M.

Richards, Mary. S. Bristol Mar 1738 AT Aug 1739. G.

Richards, Mary wife of John. SQS Bristol Feb TB to Va Mar 1771. G.
Richardson, Dawney of Etton, spinster. SQS Beverley Christmas 1759. Y.
Richardson, John. S Bristol May TB to Md Aug 1769. G.
Richardson, William. S Summer 1726 R Jun 1727. No.
Richardson, William. S Bristol Jan 1728 T *Expedition* from Bristol to South Carolina. G.
• Richardson, William. R Apr T 14 yrs Dec 1771 *Justitia*. Sy.
Rickaby, Thomas of Beverley, sailor. SQS Beverley Easter 1738. Y.
Ricketts, Elizabeth, singlewoman. S Bristol Jun AT Sep 1744 & Apr 1745. G
• Rickets, Thomas. S Mar R Jun T 14 yrs Dec 1758 *The Brothers*. E.
• Rickets, William. S Mar R Jun T 14 yrs Dec 1758 *The Brothers*. E.
• Rider, William. S Lent R Jly T 14 yrs Sep 1764 *Justitia*. E.
• Riddlesden, William. R for America Aug 1715; found at large & T Oct 1720 *Gilbert*; again found at large in Jun 1723 when he petitioned to T himself. M.
Ridman, William of North Somercoates. R for America Jly 1716. Li.
Rigglesworth, William (1774). *See* White. M.
• Riley, Ann. TB Apr 1771 *Thornton* but taken from ship & pardoned same month. Sy.
Riley, William. S Bristol Aug 1753. G.
Ringrose, John. SQS Hull Mar 1760. Y.
• Roach, John. S Dec 1761 TB *Dolphin* but R for Army service in Jamaica Jan 1762. M.
Roaden, William. S Bristol Mar 1750. G.
Roberts, Abraham. S Bristol Mar 1751. G.
Roberts *alias* Smith, Christopher of St. Andrew Holborn. R Jun 1714 & to remain in Newgate until transported. M.
Roberts, Elizabeth, singlewoman. S Bristol Mar AT Apr 1748. G.
Roberts, Henry. R 14 yrs Jun 1768. Co.
Roberts, John the elder. S Bristol Apr 1739. G.
Roberts, John the younger. S Bristol Apr 1739. G.
Roberts, Lovell of St. John Baptist. S Bristol Sep 1752. G.
Roberts, Margaret, wife of Philip, hooper. S Bristol Feb 1740. G.
Roberts, Sarah wife of William. R 14 yrs Bristol Sep 1746. G.
Roberts, Sarah (1768). *See* Lane. L.
Robarts, Thomas. S Lent R Jly 1726. De.
Roberts, William. SQS Summer 1768. Sh.
Roberts, William. SQS Bristol Apr TB to Md May 1770. G.
Robertson, John. SQS Bristol Feb TB to Md May 1770. G.
Robertson, Mary, spinster. S Bristol Sep 1728 T *Expedition* from Bristol to South Carolina. G.
• Robins, James. S Summer 1726 R 14 yrs Jly 1727. So.
• Robins, John. S Lent R 14 yrs Jun 1744 TB to Va 1745. De.

- Robinson, Benjamin. S Dec 1773 but pardoned Feb 1774. M.
Robinson, John. R 14 yrs Bristol Sep 1746. G.
- Robinson, John. S Jan-Feb but taken from ship & pardoned Apr 1774. M.
Robinson, Mary wife of John of St. Olave Southwark. R for Barbados or Jamaica Mar 1709. Sy.
- Robinson, Michael. S Summer & TB *Prince William* but R to serve in 49th Regiment in Jamaica Jly 1762. L.
Robinson, Richard. S Summer R Nov 1728. Ca.
- Robotham, George. S for killing deer at Uttoxeter Lent but R for Army service in Jamaica Apr 1762. St.
- Robson, John. S Summer 1746 R 14 yrs Summer 1747. Nl.
Robson, Richard. S Bristol Nov 1737. G.
Rogers, Ann. SQS Bristol Feb TB to Md Apr 1760. G.
Rogers, Hester. S Bristol Nov 1748. G.
Rogers, Jonathan. R Feb 1721. De.
Rogers, Mary wife of Thomas. SQS Hull & TB Aug 1757. Y.
Rogers, Thomas. R Jan 1767. St.
Rogers, William. R 14 yrs Feb 1764. Sy.
- Rolfe, Mary. S for murder of her bastard child Summer 1740 R Feb T 14 yrs Apr 1741 *Speedwell* or *Mediterranean*. Sx.
- Rolfe, Thomas. S Summer 1733 R Feb T Apr 1734 *Patapsco*. Ht.
Rooke, William. S Lent R 14 yrs Jly 1746. Ca.
- Root, George. S Feb TB *Ann* but pardoned Mar 1765. M.
Rose, Stephen. S Lent R 14 yrs Jun 1749. Sx.
Rotherford, Robert of Leicester. R for America Feb 1718. Le.
- Roundy, David. S Summer 1743 R Feb T 14 yrs May 1744 *Justitia*. Sy.
Routton, John of Tattershall, Lincs, mariner. SQS Hull Easter TB Apr 1758. Y.
Rowcastle, Christopher. S Lent R 14 yrs Jun 1744. Do.
- Rowden, Thomas. S Summer 1737 R Feb T 14 yrs Jun 1738 *Forward*. E.
Rowe, Mary of Whitechapel, spinster. R for Barbados May 1664. M.
- Rowland, Thomas. S Lent 1773; order for his release received after ship had sailed. Db.
Rudgeway, John. S Bristol Apr 1729. G.
Rumsey *alias* Smith, Ann of St. Saviour Southwark, spinster. R for Barbados or Jamaica Mar 1709. Sy.
Rumsey, Richard. S 14 yrs Bristol & TB to Md Apr 1764. G.
- Russell, George of St. Martin in Fields. SW Jun 1775 but pardoned same month. M.
- Russell, John. TB Apr 1762 *Neptune* but R for Army service in Jamaica same month. Sy.
Russell, Robert. R 14 yrs Bristol Apr 1742. G.
Russell, Stephen. S Bristol Jan AT Feb 1743. G.

- Russell, William. S Summer 1741 R 14 yrs Feb 1742. Sy.
- Rutherford, John. S Summer but R for Army Aug 1761; pardoned Jly 1764. Cu.
- Rutlidge, Thomas. S & TB Dec 1770 *Justitia* but taken from ship & R for sea service same month. M.
- Rutley, Robert. S Summer 1757 R 14 yrs Lent 1758 T Apr 1760 *Thetis*. Sx.
- Rutt, John. S Summer 1733 R 14 yrs Jun 1734. Ha.
- Rutter *alias* Asplin, Minah. SQS Summer 1775; found at large in Shrewsbury & R. Sh.
- Rutter, Thomas. S & TB Jan *Tryal* but pardoned Apr 1767. M.

Ryan, James. SQS Bristol Sep 1771 TB to Va Feb 1772. G.
- Ryan, John. S Bristol Apr R 14 yrs & TB to Va May 1774. G.
- Ryan, Mary. R 14 yrs Jly 1750. M.

Ryan, Michael, weaver. S Bristol Jan 1739. G.

- Saires, Edward. S Summer 1734 R Feb T 14 yrs Apr 1735 *Patapsco*. Sx.

Saise, Elizabeth. S (Bristol) Jun 1722 AT Apr 1723. G.

Saies, Thomas, carpenter. S Bristol Dec 1735. G.

Salloway *alias* Westwood, John. S 14 yrs Bristol for receiving & TB to Md Apr 1764. G.

Salloway, Robert. S Bristol Feb R 14 yrs Mar TB to Md Apr 1765. G.
- Sallows, Robert. S Lent R Jly T 14 yrs Sep 1742 *Forward*. E.

Salmon, Benjamin. SQS Jan 1774. Su.

Salt, Elizabeth wife of Samuel, carpenter. S Bristol Jly 1745. G.

Sampson, Ambrose (1730). *See* Chapple. So.

Sampson, John. SQS Bristol Sep 1766 TB to Md Apr 1767. G.

Sansom, Edmond. S Bristol Feb 1750. G.

Sansum, William. S Bristol Jun AT Sep 1744. G.

Santon, John. S Bristol Sep 1733. G.
- Sasser, John. S Summer 1742 R Feb T 14 yrs Apr 1743 *Justitia* but died on passage. E.
- Saul, John. S s horse Aug R 14 yrs Summer 1726 [*not 1729*]. Cu.

Saunders, Arminal, spinster. S Bristol Nov 1750. G.

Saunders, Elizabeth. S Bristol Mar 1737. G.

Saunders, John of St. Stephen's. S Bristol Feb AT Apr 1752. G.
- Saunders, John. R Jun 1768 TB to Va 1768. De.

Saunders, John. R Nov 1769. Do.
- Saunders *alias* Basely, Thomas. S Lent R 14 yrs Jly 1724. Co.

Savage, Isaac of Beverley. SQS Beverley Summer 1772. Y.

Savage, Richard. R to T himself 14 yrs Aug 1770. Ht.

Savill, George. R Jun 1714 & to remain in Newgate until transported. L.
- Sawyer, Thomas. S Dec 1766 but removed from ship at Bristol & pardoned Mar 1767. G.

Scade, James. S Aug 1748 for murder R 14 yrs Jun 1729. Du.
Scammel, Jane. R 14 yrs Bristol Mar 1736. G.
- Scammell, John. S Mar TB to Va Apr 1762 but pardoned same month. Wi.
- Scandrett, Henry. SQS Oct 1766 TB *Thornton* but removed from ship & pardoned May 1767. M.

Scandridge, Ann. S Bristol Mar AT Apr 1748. G.
- Scarr, William. S Apr but pardoned May 1775. M.

Scates, Thomas the younger. S (Bury St. Edmunds) Jan 1775. Su.
Scawen, Elizabeth. S Bristol Mar TB to Md Apr 1765. G.
Scholes, James of Hull. R for Barbados, Africa or America Feb 1696. Y.
- Schlutingt, Claus. S Feb but R for sea service Mar 1761. M.

Scott, Grizell wife of Stephen. S Summer 1748 R May 1749. Nl.
Scott, James. S Exeter Oct 1763 for assault R Feb 1764. De.
Scott, John. R yrs Nov 1769. Ha.
- Scott, Thomas. R Aug T for life Sep 1755 *Tryal*. L.

Scratton, Stephen. S Summer 1740 R 14 yrs Feb 1741. E.
Scriven, Robert. R for Barbados May 1664. L.
- Scriven, Thomas. S for perjury Summer 1760 but R for Army service Jly 1761. St.
- Sears, Giles. S Lent R Jly T Dec 1734 *Caesar*. Sy.

Sedgwick, John of Farley, husbandman. R for Barbados Jly 1671. Ha.
Seed, Thomas. S Bristol Sep 1726 AT Aug 1727. G.
Seley, Robert. R May 1731. So.
Sepper, Samuel. S Bristol Feb 1737. G.
Serjeant, Elizabeth. SQS Bristol Oct 1761 TB to Md Oct 1762. G.
Severn, Thomas. S Bristol Mar 1738. G.
Shackerly, Henry. R Apr 1723. Sy.
- Shadwell, John. S Jan TB *Tryal* but R to T himself Dec 1764. L.

Shakleton, Thomas. R 14 yrs Jun 1765. Sx.
Shapland *alias* Smith, John. S Bristol for forgery Aug R for life & TB Sep 1769 LC Georgia [undated] from *Industry*. G.
Shard, John. S Lent R Jly 1728. Wa.
Shaw, Jeremiah. S Bristol Apr 1752. G.
Shaw, Thomas. S Summer 1764 R 14 yrs Jan 1765. Sx.
Shaw, William. S Lent R 14 yrs Jly 1747. Hu.
- Sheffield, Joseph. S May but R for Army service Sep 1761. M.

Sheldon, Mary. S Lent for shoplifing R Jun 1726. Be.
- Shelly, Thomas. S Lent R 14 yrs Jly 1727. Ha.
- Shelton, Jonah. S Lent T Apr 1758 *Lux* from London. Db.
- Shepherd, Conrad. S Oct but removed from ship & pardoned Dec 1773. L.
- Sheppard, David. S Bristol May 1768 R 14 yrs & TB to Md Aug 1769. G.

- Sheppard, Robert. S Apr 1774 but taken from ship & pardoned same month. M.
  Sheres, John. R 14 yrs for highway robbery Feb 1764. K.
- Sherston, John. S Summer 1742 R Feb T 14 yrs Apr 1743 *Justitia*. Ht.
- Shields, Elizabeth, spinster. S Bristol Apr R 14 yrs & TB to Va Jly 1772. G.
- Shin *alias* Slim, Abraham. SW & TB *Scarsdale* Jun 1771 but taken from ship & pardoned same month. M.
  Shugar, Sarah, spinster. SQS Bristol Sep 1768 TB to Md Apr 1769. G.
- Silver, William. S Mar R Jun T 14 yrs Sep 1758 *Tryal*. Sy.
  Silverthorne, Hester. S Bristol Jan AT Feb 1743. G.
- Silvester, Richard. R Jly T 14 yrs Sep 1764 *Justitia*. Sy.
- Silvester, Thomas. SQS Apr but pardoned May 1773. M.
- Simpson, Anne. S City Summer 1746 R 14 yrs Summer 1747. Nl.
- Simpson, James. S for forging will & R 14 yrs Summer 1760; pardoned for Army service Mar 1762. Du.
- Simpson, Jonathan. S Feb but R for sea service Mar 1761. M.
  Simpson, Thomas of Shipton. SQS Beverley Easter 1747. Y.
- Simpson, William. S Summer 1728 R 14 yrs Feb 1731. Wi.
- Singleton, Bridget. S Feb but pardoned Apr 1773. L.
- Sircomb, Thomas. S Summer 1730 R 14 yrs May 1731 TB to Va. De.
  Sizer, William. S Summer 1741 R 14 yrs Feb 1742. Nf.
  Skelton, Elizabeth. SL Aug T Oct 1760 *Phoenix*. Sy.
- Skillard *alias* Killard, William. R Jun 1768 TB to Va 1768. De.
  Skinner, Jane. S Bristol Feb AT Aug 1749. G.
  Skinner, William. S Bristol Oct 1744. G.
  Skuse, Edward of Tinhead, Westbury, husbandman. R for America Jly 1696. Wi.
  Slade, Samuel. SQS Bristol Mar TB to Va May 1775. G.
  Slim, Abraham (1771). *See* Shin. M.
  Sloman, William. S Summer 1741 R 14 yrs Feb 1742. Sx.
  Smith, Abraham. R 14 yrs Bristol May 1761. G.
- Smith, Andrew. R Feb T Sep 1730 *Smith*. E.
  Smith, Ann (1709). *See* Rumsey. Sy.
  Smith, Anne, spinster. S Bristol Mar 1742. G.
  Smith, Anne, widow. S Bristol Apr 1743. G.
  Smith *alias* Hewling, Ann, spinster. SQS Bristol Feb TB to Va Mar 1771. G.
  Smith, Benjamin. SQS Hull Epiphany TB Jan 1770. Y.
- Smith, Charles. S Oct 1761 but R for Army service same month. L.
  Smith, Christopher (1714). *See* Roberts. M.
  Smith, Daniel. S Lent R Jly 1734. Sy.
  Smith, Elias. SQS s shoes Oct 1770. Sh.
  Smith, Elizabeth. R 14 yrs Bristol Apr 1737. G.
  Smith, Elizabeth. S Bristol Apr 1739

Smith, Elizabeth, spinster. S Bristol Mar 1753. G.
- Smith, Elizabeth. R Summer 1773, found pregnant, removed from ship on appeal of mother & pardoned Dec 1773. Sy.
- Smith, Francis. S for killing deer at Uttoxeter Lent but R for Army service Apr 1762. St.
- Smith, George. R 14 yrs Aug 1767 but pardoned same month. Wi.
- Smith, Henry. S Mar 1762 but R for Army service same month. Ha.
- Smith, Henry, *alias* Johnson, William. R Apr T Dec 1771 *Justitia*. Sx.
- Smith, Humfrey. S Summer 1730 R 14 yrs Feb 1731. Wi.
- Smith, James. S Jan & TB *Dolphin* but R for Army Feb 1762. M.
- Smith, James. S & TB Mar *Tryal* but pardoned May 1764. L.

Smith, Jane, spinster. S Bristol Apr 1752. G.

Smith, John. S Oct R Nov 1728. Ca.
- Smith, John. S Summer 1733 R Jun 1734. So.
- Smith, John. S Lent R Jly T 14 yrs Sep 1742 *Forward*. Ht.

Smith, John. S Bristol Apr AT Sep 1744. G.
- Smith, John of Rotherhithe, grocer. S Mar TB Jly 1758 *Tryal* but pardoned same month for sea service. Sy.

Smith, John. S Bristol Aug 1758 R 14 yrs Aug TB to Md Sep 1759. G.

Smith, John (1759). *See* Jones. Db.

Smith, John. SQS Summer 1766. G.

Smith, John (1769). *See* Shapland. G.

Smith, Mary wife of John, hooper. S Bristol Mar 1742. G.

Smith, Michael. S Bristol Mar 1741. G.

Smith, Rachel wife of William. S Bristol Mar 1742. G.

Smith, Richard of Hollingbourne. R for Barbados or Jamaica Mar 1709. K.

Smith, Robert, mariner. S Bristol Aug 1736. G.
- Smith, Robert. S & TB Dec 1769 *Justitia* but R to T himself Mar 1770. L.

Smith, Simon. S Bristol Mar 1741. G.
- Smith, Thomas. T *Expedition* from Bristol to South Carolina 1728. Wo.
- Smith, Thomas. S Aug 1757 R Jun T 14 yrs Dec 1758 *The Brothers*. K.
- Smith, Thomas. S Lent but R for Army service Apr 1761. E.

Smith, Thomas of Kilnwick. SQS Beverley Christmas 1764. Y.

Smith, Thomas. R for life Feb 1767. G.

Smith, William. R Jun 1714 & to remain in Newgate until transported. L.
- Smith, William. R Jan T Feb 1726 *Supply* LC Annapolis May 1726. K.
- Smith, William, *alias* Turner, John. R Jly 1763 in Mddx.; executed in Aug 1770 for returning. Bu.

Smith, William. SQS Bristol Aug TB to Md Sep 1763. G.

Smith, William (1768). *See* Johnson, Robert. Y.

- Smith, William. S for forgery at Houghton le Spring & R for life Summer 1769 T *Caesar* but shipwrecked & pardoned for sea service Feb 1771. Du.
- Smithers, Ann. S Feb 1773 but pardoned same month. L.
- Smithson, John. S Mar 1761 but R for sea service same month. L.

  Snarbaum, Jacob. R to T himself for life Feb 1770. L.
- Snell, James. R 14 yrs Apr 1769 TB to Va 1769. De.
- Snell, Thomas. R Jun T 14 yrs Dec 1758 *The Brothers*. K.
- Sockett, Martha. S Summer but pardoned Oct 1773. Sy.
- Solme, Jacob. S Summer 1740 R Feb T 14 yrs Apr 1741 *Speedwell* or *Mediterranean*. E.
- Solomon, Isaac. S May TB *Prince William* but R to serve in Army in Jamaica Jly 1762. M.

  Solowin, Margaret. R for life Feb 1762. LM.
- Soul, Thomas. S & R 14 yrs Lent 1773 [*not 1763*]. G.
- South, Thomas. S Lent R 14 yrs Jun 1744. Ha.
- Sparey *alias* Parry, John. S Lent R 14 yrs Summer 1767; ordered to be kept in custody pending appeal but ordered for T Sep 1767. St.

  Sparkes, James. R for Barbados or Jamaica Aug 1700. L.
- Sparks, Mary. S Lent R 14 yrs Jun 1734. Do.
- Sparkman, Samuel. S Feb R 14 yrs Jly 1758. Ha.
- Sparrow *alias* Broughton, William. S Aug 1752; found at large but R for sea service Oct 1757. So.
- Spencer, John. S Lent 1773; order for release of May 1773 made after his ship had sailed. Db.

  Sprainger, Richard. S Summer 1729 R Feb 1730. K

  Sprout, Joseph. R Feb 1766 s mare. St.

  Stacey, Thomas. S (Bury St. Edmunds) Jan 1775. Su.

  Stackable, Paul. S Bristol Aug 1753. G.

  Stafford, Ann. S 14 yrs Bristol & TB to Md Apr 1764. G.
- Stafford, Thomas Jr. S Lent but R for Army service May 1756. Bu.

  Stamer, Elizabeth. S Lent 1769. Li.

  Standred, Eustace. R (Chester Circuit) for Barbados Nov 1666. X.
- Stanley *alias* Alder, Ann. S Jly TB *Justitia* but ordered to remain ashore Aug 1765. M.

  Stanley, Daniel. SQS Summer 1775. St.

  Stanley, George. S Bristol May TB to Md Aug 1769. G.

  Stanley, William SQS Lent 1774. Sh.
- Stannard, Stephen. SEK & TB Dec 1771 *Justitia* but pardoned Jun 1772. K.

  Stater, Francis. SQS s iron Jly 1773. Sh.

  Stedman, William. R for Barbados May 1664. L.

  Steed, Joshua. S (Bristol) Dec 1721. G.

  Steel, John. R for life Jly 1762. Sy.

- Stelfox, Sarah. S 14 yrs for receiving Lent 1771 but pardoned May 1773. La.
Stevens, Robert of Stratfield, husbandman. R for Barbados Jly 1671. Ha.
- Stevens *alias* Marshall, Sarah of Stepney, spinster. R for America May 1704 [*not 1774*]. M.
Stephens, Thomas. R 14 yrs Apr 1773. Wo.
Stephens, William. SQS Bristol Dec 1767 TB to Md Apr 1768. G.
Stephenson, Humphrey of Enfield. R for Barbados Sep 1677. M.
Stephenson, Samuel. SQS Hull Michaelmas TB Nov 1766. Y.
- Stevenson, William. S s at St. Michael Lent 1761 T *Atlas* from Bristol; pardoned for Army service Jly 1761. St.
Sterling, John. S Bristol Aug 1732. G.
Steward, Elianor. S Summer 1727 R Jly 1728. Wa.
Steward, Stephen. SQS (Bury St. Edmunds) Jan 1774. Su.
Steward, William. SQS Bristol Jun TB to Md Oct 1762. G.
Stewart, Elizabeth wife of James. SQS Bristol Dec 1773 TB to Va May 1774.
Stewart, Hugh. S Bristol Aug 1753. G.
Steuart, John. SQS Bristol Jun TB to Md Sep 1766 LC Annapolis from *Randolph* Mar 1767. G.
- Stiff, John. SQS Oct 1761 TB *Dolphin* but R for Army service Feb 1762. M.
- Stockbridge, Herbert. S Summer but R for Army Aug 1761. Cu.
Stokes, Ann wife of William. SQS Hull Easter 1772. Y.
- Stokes, Jacob [*not Joseph*]. S Lent R 14 yrs Jun 1734. Wi.
Stokes, William. SQS Bristol Jly AT Aug 1775. G.
- Stolery, Brice. S Jly 1757 R Feb T 14 yrs Sep 1758 *Tryal*. E.
Stone, Thomas of St. Thomas's. S Bristol Feb AT Apr 1752. G.
Stone, William. S Bristol Oct 1744. G.
Stourt *alias* Stuart, John. R 14 yrs Aug 1773. M.
Stowell, Caleb. S Jly 1728 T *Expedition* from Bristol to South Carolina. G.
Stratton, Birton. S Bristol Nov 1748. G.
- Stratton, William Jr. S for rape at Sporle Summer 1773 R 14 yrs Summer 1775; then to hang for being at large. Nf.
- Stream, John. SQS Oct TB Nov 1771 *Justitia* but pardoned same month. M.
Stretton, John of Derby[shire]. R for America Feb 1696. Db.
Strickland, Elizabeth wife of George. SQS Bristol Jun 1771 TB to Va Feb 1772. G.
- Strickland [*not Brickland*], Richard. R for America Aug 1715. M.
Stringer, Robert. R 14 yrs Feb 1762. No.
Stroud, Bernard. S (Bristol) Dec 1721. G.
- Strude, William. S Lent R Jly T Sep 1764 *Justitia*. K.
- Strudwick, Thomas. S Apr R Sep T 14 yrs Dec 1771 *Justitia*. Sy.

Stuart, John (1773). *See* Stourt. M.
- Sturgeon, John. S Summer 1738 R Feb T 14 yrs Apr 1739 *Forward*. Ht.

Styles, George. S Summer 1752 R Feb 1753. Ha.

Sugg, Charles. SQS Bristol Dec 1771 TB to Va Feb 1772. G.

Sullivan *alias* O'Sullivan, Bryan of Islington. R for Barbados or Jamaica Aug 1700. M.

Summers, Robert. R 14 yrs Apr 1771. G.
- Sumner, William. S s clocks at New Windsor Lent 1773; appeal rejected but R to T himself Apr 1773. Be.

Sutherland, Mary, spinster. SQS Bristol Dec 1773 TB to Va May 1774. G.

Sutton, Benjamin. S Apr R Jly 1752. St.

Sutton, Joseph. S Mar R 14 yrs Jun 1759. E.

Swayne [*not Drayne*], Thomas of Ashfield. R Jly 1703. Su.

Swayne, William. S Lent R 14 yrs Jun 1744. Ha.
- Swaine, William. S Summer 1764 R May T 14 yrs Sep 1765 *Justitia*. Sx.

Sweeny, John. S Bristol Aug 1758 for assisting an escape from prison. G.

Sweeney, Mary. S Bristol Apr 1767 TB to Md Sep 1768. G.

Sweet, William. SQS Bristol Jun 1760 TB to Md Apr 1761. G.
- Sweetman, John. R May T 14 yrs Sep 1767 *Justitia*. Sx.
- Swigg, William. R 14 yrs Aug 1760 but R for Army service Jly 1761. Co.

Symes or Symms, Elizabeth, singlewoman. R 14 yrs Bristol Sep 1745. G.
- Symes *alias* White, John. R 14 yrs Apr 1769 TB to Va 1769. De.
- Symes, Thomas. S Lent R 14 yrs Jun 1744. So.
- Symonds, John. S Lent 1734 R 14 yrs Feb 1735. So.
- Symons, John. S Summer 1740 R 14 yrs Feb 1741. So.

Symmons, Thomas. S Bristol Oct 1753. G.

Symonds, William (1771). *See* Hunt. He.

Sytron, William. S Summer 1734 R 14 yrs Feb 1735. K.

Taberer, Philip. S Bristol Nov 1750. G.

Talbot, Elizabeth. S Bristol Feb AT Sep 1744 & Apr 1745. G.

Tanner, John. SQS Bristol Feb TB to Md Apr 1768. G.

Taplin, Samuel. S Bristol Mar 1742. G.
- Tapp, Richard. R Nov 1769 TB to Va 1770. De.

Tapp, Thomas of Stoke St. Gregory. R for Barbados Feb 1671. So.
- Tarbock, George. S Summer 1750 R 14 yrs Feb 1751. La.

Tarrat, James. R 14 yrs Apr 1769. Ha.
- Taylor, Edward. S Summer 1734 R Feb T 14 yrs Apr 1735 *Patapsco*. Sy.

Taylor, Edward. S Summer 1752 R Feb 1753. So.
- Taylor, Francis. S Summer 1730 R 14 yrs Feb 1731. So.

- Taylor, George of Nottingham. R for America Feb 1713 & Jun 1714. Nt.
Taylor, George (1761). *See* Gill. Le.
- Taylor, James. TB 14 yrs Mar 1767 *Thornton* but pardoned same month. Ht.
Taylor, John. S Bristol Jun 1726. G.
- Taylor, Richard. R Dec 1766 but pardoned Feb 1767. G.
- Taylor, Robert. S Mar but pardoned Jun 1761. Ha.
- Taylor, Samuel. SQS Apr but pardoned May 1773. M.
Taylor, Susannah, singlewoman. S Bristol Jan 1741. G.
- Taylor, Thomas. S Lent R 14 yrs May 1733. De.
- Taylor, Thomas. S Lent but R to serve in 49th Regiment in Jamaica Apr 1761. Sy.
Taylor, Thomas. R to be T for life Apr 1773. E.
Taylor, William of Hartley Wintney. R for America Jly 1696. Ha.
- Taylor *alias* Barrett, William. S Lent R 14 yrs May TB to Va Aug 1731. Wi.
- Taylor, William. R Feb T 14 yrs Jun 1764 *Dolphin*. K.
- Taylor, William. R Jun T 14 yrs Sep 1766 *Justitia*. E.
- Taylor, William. S Apr TB Jly 1770 *Scarsdale* but pardoned same month. M.
Taylton, Mary wife of John of St. Saviour, Southwark. R for Barbados or Jamaica Jly 1715. Sy.
Teague, Eliza, singlewoman. S Bristol Sep 1730. G.
Teakle, William. R 14 yrs Apr 1771. G.
Tenny, William. S Summer 1742 R 14 yrs Feb 1743. E.
Tepper, Sampson. R for forging money order Jan 1738. De.
Thomas, David. SQS Bristol Aug TB to Md Sep 1766 LC Annapolis from *Randolph* Mar 1767. G.
Thomas *alias* Phillips, David. S Bristol for returning from T May R for life & TB to Md Aug 1769. G.
Thomas *alias* Williams, David. S Bristol Apr R 7 yrs & TB to Va Jly 1772. G.
Thomas, Elizabeth, spinster. S Bristol Aug 1743. G.
Thomas, Elizabeth wife of William. S Bristol Apr R 14 yrs & TB to Va Jly 1772. G.
Thomas, Evan. S Bristol Lent R Jly 1723. G.
Thomas, Francis. SQS Bristol & TB to Md Sep 1770. G.
Thomas, George. SQS Bristol & TB May 1769 LC Rappahannock from *Brickdale* Aug 1769. G.
Thomas, Griffith. S Bristol Nov 1749. G.
Thomas, Jenkin. S Bristol Jan AT Apr 1743. G.
Thomas, John of Stepney. R for Barbados or Jamaica Aug 1700. M.
- Thomas, John. S Lent R 14 yrs Jun 1734. So.
Thomas, John of Hull, yeoman. SQS Hull Dec 1758 TB Jan 1759. Y.
Thomas, Mary, singlewoman. S Bristol Aug 1741. G.

Thomas, Robert of Swanscombe. R for Barbados Jun 1671. K.
Thomas, Robert. SQS Bristol Nov 1771 TB to Va Feb 1772. G.
Thomas *alias* Price, Susannah, spinster. SQS Bristol Dec 1770 TB to Va Mar 1771. G.
Thomas, Thomas, brickmaker. S Bristol Jan 1739. G.
Thomas, William (1736). *See* Beer, Hugh.
- Thomas, William. S Mar 1761 TB to Va but R for Army service Aug 1761. De.
- Thompson, Alice. S Feb 1761 but pardoned same month. L.
- Thompson, Cuthbert, aged 19. R for life for highway robbery on appeal of Mayor of Newcastle Summer 1765. Nl.
Thompson, Eleanor wife of John of Hull, schoolmaster. SQS Hull Easter TB Apr 1758. Y.
Thompson, Margaret. SQS Hull Easter 1749. Y.
Thompson, Mary (1721). *See* Wergiam. De.
Thompson, Mary wife of Isaac. SQS Hull Easter 1753. Y.
- Thompson, Richard. S May 1760 but R for Army service Jun 1761. M.
Thompson, Robert, aged 35, pitman. S Lent 1774 but in Morpeth Prison in Dec 1775. Nl.
Thompson, Thomas. S for cutting trees in a plantation Summer 1752 R Feb 1753. Ha.
Thompson, William of Falmouth. R for America Jly 1696. Co.
- Thompson, William. T *Expedition* from Bristol to South Carolina 1728. Wo.
Tomson, William. R 7 yrs Apr 1774. Wa.
Thorn, William. R Feb 1720. LM.
Thornton, Ann wife of John of Hull, blockmaker. SQS Hull Epiphany 1759 TB Sep 1760. Y.
- Thorpe, William. R Feb T 14 yrs Nov 1762 *Prince William*. E.
- Thorrington, John. S Summer 1743 R Feb T 14 yrs May 1744 *Justitia*. K.
- Thredgall, John. S Lent R Jly T Dec 1736 *Dorsetshire*. E.
Thrift, John. R 14 yrs for murder May 1750. L.
- Throup, James. S & TB Jly *Scarsdale* but R to T himself Aug 1771. M.
- Tibbs, John. S Mar for rape R Jun T 14 yrs Nov 1759 *Phoenix*. Sy.
- Tibbs, William of St. Mary le Bow. R for America Aug 1715. M.
Tidbury, Joseph. S Oct R 14 yrs Dec 1774. LM.
Tiggall, Thomas (1741). *See* Tigwell. Ha.
- Tigwell *alias* Tiggall, Thomas. S Summer 1741 R 14 yrs Feb 1742. Ha.
Tilbury, William. R for life Nov 1769. Ha.
Tiley, Hannah. R Jan 1737 for shoplifting. Ha.
- Till, William. S & TB Sep 1765 *Justitia* but taken from ship & R to T himself. M.
- Tillaboo, John, a negro. S Bristol Apr 1771 LC Granada from *Mercury* Mar 1772.

Tilletts, Samuel. S Bristol Oct 1744. G.
Tilletts, Samuel. S Bristol Jan 1750. G.
Tillin, Thomas. R 14 yrs Jun 1768. Wi.
Timbrell, John. S Lent R Jun 1726. Be.
- Timer *alias* Timewell, Ann. S Summer 1746 R 14 yrs Feb 1747. De.
Timewell, Ann (1746). *See* Timer. De.
Tindall *alias* Wood, Ann of Leconfield. SQS Beverley Summer 1758. Y.
- Tinson, Duke. S Summer 1730 R 14 yrs Feb 1731. Wi.
Tipler, William (1727). *See* Tipling. De.
Tipling *alias* Tipler, William. S Lent R Jly 1727. De.
- Tipper, James. S Summer 1746 R 14 yrs Feb 1747. De.
- Tipper, John. S Lent R Jly T 14 yrs Sep 1742 *Forward*. K.
Tire, Michael. S Bristol Mar 1742. G.
- Tisely, John. S Summer 1764 R Jan 1765; found at large & R Jun T for life Sep 1766 *Justitia*. K.
Tite, Walter. S Bristol May TB to Md Aug 1769. G.
- Tiverton, Joseph. R Jun T 14 yrs Sep 1766 *Justitia*. E.
- Todd *alias* Hudspeth, William. S s books Summer 1769 T *Caesar* but shipwrecked & R for sea service Dec 1770. Nl.
Toker, John. S Lent R 14 yrs Jun 1764. E.
- Tolhurst, John. R Jun T 14 yrs Sep 1766 *Justitia*. K.
Tomkin, Gabriel. T delayed for him to confess accomplices but now to be T Feb 1722. LM.
- Tomlin, William. S Lent R Jun T 14 yrs Jly 1723 *Alexander* LC Md Sep 1723. Bu.
- Tomkyns, Thomas. S s beans & peas at Wroxton Summer but pardoned Aug 1757. O.
Tomlinson, George. R 14 yrs Jly 1771. Nl.
Tongue, John. S Bristol May TB to Md Sep 1763. G.
Tonge, Sarah. R to T herself 7 yrs May 1773. L or M.
Took, James. R 14 yrs Bristol Aug 1748. G.
Toole, James. S Bristol Apr R May 1748. G.
- Towning, William. R Jun 1768 TB to Va 1768. De.
Towse, Francis. SQS Hull Easter TB May 1770. Y.
- Townsend, William. S s at South Cerney Lent 1768; pardoned May 1768 but ship had already left. G.
- Tracey, George. S Lent R Jun T 14 yrs Oct 1738 *Genoa*. K.
Trapnell, George. SQS Bristol Aug 1771 TB to Va Feb 1772. G.
Trapp, Thomas. S Bristol Mar 1741. G.
- Trask, Susannah wife of Samuel. R Apr 1769 TB to Va 1769. De.
Tredinnick, William (1752). *See* Dinnick. De.
- Tregowith, John. S Jly 1760 but R for sea service Jun 1761. De.
Trehane, William of Walkhampton, husbandman. R for America Jly 1696. De.
Trellego, Arthur (1731). *See* Trevaseus. Co.

- Tremble, George. TB 14 yrs Apr 1768 *Thornton* but taken from ship & R to enlist in East India Co. Sy.
- Trevaseus *alias* Trelleggo, Arthur. S Summer for highway robbery 1730 R Feb 1731. Co.
- Trevit, John. S Summer 1752 R Feb 1753. Do.
- Trickey [*not Truckey*], Joseph of Hackney. R for Barbados or Jamaica Aug 1701. M.
- Trigg, John (1723). *See* Fogg. E.
- Trippus [*not Trippup*], John of Kingston on Thames. R for Barbados or Jamaica Feb 1719. Sy.
- Trottle or Throttle, Robert. S for Va Jly 1718; found at large & appealed for pardon Jun 1721. Do.
- Truelock, Giles of Bermondsey. SQS Oct 1761 but R for Army service same month. Sy.
- Trump, Richard. S Summer R Feb T 14 yrs Apr 1741 *Speedwell* or *Mediterranean*. Sx.
- Tucker, Joseph. S Oct but pardoned Nov 1772. L.
- Tucker, William. SQS Bristol Sep 1774 TB to Va May 1775. G.
- Tully, William. S Bristol Aug 1749. G.
- Turbut, Benjamin Robert. R to T himself for life Oct 1765. L.
- Turner, John (1742). *See* Turner, Richard. K.
- Turner, John (1763). *See* Smith, William. Bu.
- Turner, John. SQS Bristol Feb TB to Md Apr 1768. G.
- Turner, Joseph. SQS Bristol Dec 1767 TB to Md Apr 1768. G.
- Turner, Richard *alias* John. S Lent R Jly T 14 yrs Sep 1742 *Forward*. K.
- Twist, Mary. S (Bristol) Apr 1722 AT Apr 1723. G.
- Twynam, William. SQS Lent 1772. O
- Tyer, John. S Lent R Jly T Sep 1764 *Justitia*. K.

Underlin, George. SQS Bristol Dec 1765 TB to Md Apr 1766. G.
Underwood, Shadreck. SQS Bristol Mar TB to Md May 1763. G.
- Urvoy, Toussaint Felix. S Jan for perjury TB Mar 1762 *Dolphin* but R same month for Army service in Jamaica. L.

Varin, Benjamin of Blandford Forum. R for America Jly 1696. Do.
- Vaughan, Henry. S Summer 1764 R Feb T 14 yrs Apr 1765 *Ann*. K.
Vaughan, Isaac. S Bristol Jly AT Aug 1749. G.
Vaughan, John. SQS Bristol Oct 1764 TB to Md Apr 1765. G.
- Vaughan, Richard. S s at Abbey Dore Summer 1760 T *Atlas* 1761 from Bristol; R for Army service Aug 1761. He.
Vaughan, Susan of Braintree, spinster. R for Barbados or Jamaica Mar 1709. E.

Vaughan, William. S Bristol Sep 1728 T *Expedition* from Bristol to South Carolina. G.
Venables, Eleanor. SQS Bristol Aug 1761 TB to Md Oct 1762. G.
Vennell, Richard. R for life Feb 1767. Wi.
• Verdon, Joseph. R Feb T 14 yrs Jun 1764 *Dolphin*. Sy.
Vernell, William. SQS Bristol Feb TB to Md Apr 1765. G.
• Vevers *alias* Bever, John. S Dec 1767 TB Apr 1768 *Thornton* but case reviewed Jun 1768 & again ordered for T. L.
Veysey, Thomas SQS Lent 1775. G.
Viger, George of St. Botolph Aldgate. R for Barbados May 1664. M.
Vile, Dorothy, singlewoman. R 14 yrs Bristol Sep 1745. G.
• Vince, John. S Jun TB Sep 1767 *Justitia* but pardoned on appeal of father Oct 1767. M.
Vincent, John (1764). *See* Vinson. De.
Vinson *alias* Vincent, John. R for highway robbery Feb 1764. De.
Vivyan, John. S Summer 1740 R 14 yrs Feb 1741. De.

Wackett, John. S Summer 1753 R 14 yrs Feb 1754. Le.
Waite, John. S Bristol Apr TB to Va Aug 1774. G.
Waite, Robert of Abbey Holme. R for Barbados, Africa or America Feb 1696. Cu.
• Waldron, Grace. S Lent R May 1731 TB to Va. De.
• Walker, James. S Bristol Apr R 7 yrs & TB to Va Jly 1772. G.
• Walker, Richard. S Summer 1729 R Feb T Sep 1730 *Smith*. K.
• Walker, Robert. S Jan-Feb T 14 yrs Apr 1772 *Thornton*; found at large & R for life Dec 1773. M.
Walker, Thomas. S Bristol Mar 1751. G.
Walker, William. SQS Bristol Mar TB to Md Apr 1766. G.
Wall, Henry. S Summer 1723 R Feb 1724. He.
Wall, Hugh. S Bristol Apr 1743. G.
• Wall, John. R Apr T Oct 1723 *Forward*. Sy.
Wall, John, *alias* Parker, Richard. R Jun 1737. Ht.
Wall, John. S Bristol Dec 1751. G.
• Wallace, Hendry. S Mar but R to serve in Army in Jamaica Jun 1762. De.
Wallis, Hannah, singlewoman. S Bristol Aug 1739. G.
Wallis, John. S Summer 1773. Bu.
Wallis, Thomas of Chippenham. R for Barbados May 1664. Wi.
Walls, Thomas. S Lent 1766. Bd.
• Walsham, Robert. S Summer 1741 R Feb T 14 yrs Apr 1742 *Bond*. Sy.
• Walter, Mary. T *Expedition* from Bristol to South Carolina 1728. Wi.
• Walters, Isaac. S Lent R 14 yrs Jly 1724. De.
• Walters, John. R for life Jly 1773. M.
Walters, Morgan. SQS Bristol Jly AT Aug 1775. G.

- Warbey, Edward. S Mar R Jun T 14 yrs Dec 1758 *The Brothers*. Ht.
Ward, James. R for life for highway robbery Dec 1768. So.
Ward, John. R 14 yrs Apr 1771. G.
Ward, Martha. SQS Hull Epiphany TB Oct 1765. Y.
- Ward, Thomas. S Jan-Feb but taken from ship & pardoned Apr 1775. M.
Ward, William of Fosdyke. R for America Mar 1671. Li.
- Warner, John. S Feb but R for sea service Mar 1761. M.
- Warner, Simon. SQS (Peterborough) Aug R Sep 1718. No.
Warren, Peter. R 14 yrs Bristol Sep 1749. G.
Warren, William of Cambridge. R Jly 1703. Ca.
- Washford, Mary. S Lent R Jun T 14 yrs Oct 1738 *Genoa*. Sy.
Washman, William. S Summer 1743 R 14 yrs Feb 1744. Sy.
- Waterhouse, Elizabeth. S Jly 1773 but pardoned same month. L.
- Waters, John. R & TB 14 yrs Jly 1772 *Tayloe* but taken from ship & pardoned same month. M.
Waters, Joseph (1768). *See* Williams, Thomas. Bd.
Waters, Mary (1744). *See* Marsh. G.
Waters, William. S Bristol Sep 1737. G.
Watkins, Anne, singlewoman. S Bristol Apr 1741. G.
Watkins, Ann, spinster. SQS Bristol Nov 1769 TB to Md May 1770. G.
Watkins, Elizabeth. S Bristol Aug 1750. G.
Watkins, George. S Bristol Jan 1734. G.
- Watkins, Richard. S Oct 1761 TB *Dolphin* but R for Army service same month. M.
- Watkins, Walter. S Lent R 14 yrs Summer 1760 T *Atlas* from Bristol 1761; R for Army service Aug 1761. He.
- Watson, James William. TB Apr 1771 *Thornton* but R for Army service same month. M.
- Watson, Richard. S s cloth at St. Mary, Shrewsbury, Summer but pardoned Sep 1774. Sh.
- Watson, Robert. S Apr TB Jly 1770 *Scarsdale* but R same month to T himself. M.
Watson, Thomas SQS Lent 1775. G.
- Watson, William. S Lent R Jly T 14 yrs Sep 1742 *Forward*. K.
Watton, George. R 14 yrs for shooting with intent to kill Feb 1740. K.
Watts, Solomon. R for Barbados May 1664. L.
- Wawn, John of Donington. R for America Feb 1713 & Jun 1714. Li.
Weaver, John. S Bristol May 1740. G.
Webb, John. S Bristol Jun AT Sep 1744. G.
Webb, Thomas, a boy. S Lent R Jly 1728. Wa.
Webb, William. S (Bristol) Oct 1722. G.
Webber, John. SQS Bristol Mar TB to Va May 1775. G.
Webber, William, *alias* Greenslade, John. S Aug 1753 R 14 yrs Feb 1754. De.
Weeks, John. S Bristol Mar 1740. G.

Weeks, Obediah. S Summer 1740 R 14 yrs Feb 1741. De.
- Weene, Richard [*not John*] of Colemore. R for Barbados Feb 1683. Ha.
- Welch, James. R 14 yrs Mar 1762 but R for Army service same month. Ha.
- Welch, Philip. S Dec 1772 but pardoned same month. M.

Welchman, Samuel (1722). *See* Armstrong.
- Wellar, John. S Lent R for life Summer 1758. Ha.
- Wells, James. S Summer 1741 R Feb T 14 yrs Apr 1742 *Bond*. K.

Wells, John of Newington. R for Barbados Jun 1671. Sy.
Wells, John. S Bristol Sep 1731. G.
Wells, Joseph. S Bristol Jun 1750. G.
Welsh, John. SQS 14 yrs Bristol Feb TB to Md Apr 1768. G.
Welsh, Robert. S Bristol Aug 1750. G.
- Wensley, Thomas. S Mar 1730 R 14 yrs Jun 1731. So.

Wergiam *alias* Thompson, Mary. R Feb 1721. De.
West, John of Lyneham. R for America Jly 1696. Wi.
West, John. S Jly 1758 R 14 yrs Feb 1759. Sx.
West, Margaret wife of James, weaver. S Bristol Apr 1742. G.
Westall, Henry. S May 1775. L or M.
- Westcombe, William. S Lent R Jun 1734. So.

Westear, John. R Jun 1737. O.
Westendale, John. R Jun 1726. Db.
Westlake, James. SQS Bristol Mar TB to Va May 1774. G.
Westley, Magdalen, widow. S Bristol Jun AT Sep 1745. G.
Weston, Thomas. R Nov 1769. Do.
Westwood, John (1764). *See* Salloway. G.
Wharton, Thomas. R for Barbados May 1664. L.
Whatnel, John. S Bristol Sep 1733. G.
- Wheatley *alias* Whitney, Mary. S Apr TB Jly 1770 *Scarsdale* but removed from ship & pardoned same month. M.

Wheeler, James. AT Bristol Aug 1741. G.
Wheeler, William. S Bristol Aug 1749. G.
Whitaker, John. R 14 yrs 1759, pardoned for time unexpired Jan 1771. ?Nl.
White, Charles. SQS Hull Epiphany 1774. Y.
White, Hannah of St. Martin in Fields, spinster. R for Barbados or Jamaica Aug 1700. M.
- White, Henry. S Lent R 14 yrs May 1731. So.

White, James. S Summer 1745 R 14 yrs Jan 1746. So.
White, John (1769). *See* Symes. De.
- White, Orlando. S Lent R Jly T Dec 1734 *Caesar*. E.

White, Rachel of Braintree, spinster. R for Barbados or Jamaica Mar 1709. E.
- White, Thomas. R Apr T for life Dec 1771 *Justitia*. Sy.

- White, William. TB 14 yrs Jly 1762 *Prince William* but R for Army in Jamaica same month. K.
- White *alias* Rigglesworth, William. S Sep-Oct but taken from ship & pardoned Nov 1774. M.

Whitecake, Thomas of Isle of Ely. R for Barbados Oct 1664. Ca.
- Whitehead, Daniel. S May 1715 R & T Dec 1716 *Lewis* to Jamaica. L.

Whitemesh, John. R 14 yrs Sep 1768. Ha.

Whiteing, John. S Lent R Jun 1727. Li.

Whiting, Thomas. S Summer 1743 R 14 yrs Feb 1744. Sy.
- Whiting, Thomas. S Lent R Jun T 14 yrs Oct 1738 *Genoa*. Ht.

Whitney, Mary (1770). *See* Wheatley. M.
- Whiton, John [*not Henry*]. S s calf Lent R 14 yrs Jun 1763. O.
- Wicks, Thomas. S Lent R Jun T 14 yrs Oct 1738 *Genoa*. Sx.

Wiggington, John (1772). *See* East. M.

Wilcocks, Isaac. S (Bristol) Lent 1767. G.

Whylde, Jane, spinster, *alias* wife of John. R for Barbados May 1664. L.

Wylde, Susan of Romsey. R for Barbados Feb 1671. Ha.

Wilcocks, Isaac. S Bristol & TB to Md Apr 1767. G.

Wilcox, Joseph. S Bristol Aug 1758 for assisting an escape from prison. G.
- Wilder, Thomas. R for life Aug 1737. Ha.

Wilkes, Thomas. SQS Summer 1771. St.
- Wilkins, Stephen. S Lent R 14 yrs Jly 1724. Ha.
- Wilkins, Thomas. S Summer 1742 R 14 yrs Feb 1743. So.
- Wilkins, William. S Summer 1742 R 14 yrs Feb 1743. So.
- Wilkinson, Elisha. S s ribbon at St. Mary, Huntingdon, Summer 1769; detained but to be T by next ship Jly 1770. Hu.
- Wilkinson, John of Whitechapel. R Aug 1715 T Dec 1716 *Lewis* to Jamaica. M.

Wilkinson, John. S Summer R Nov 1728. Ca.

Willett, Joseph. S Bristol Feb 1734. G.

Williams, Abigail, singlewoman. S Bristol Apr 1746. G.

Williams, Ann. SQS Bristol & TB to Md Sep 1761. G.

Williams, Ann. SQS Bristol Aug 1767 TB to Md Sep 1768. G.

Williams, Benjamin of St. Martin in the Fields. R Jun 1714 & to remain in Newgate until transported. M.

Williams, Benjamin. SQS Bristol Feb TB to Va Apr 1773. G.

Williams, Catherine of Beverley, singlewoman. SQS Beverley Summer 1739. Y.

Williams, Charles (1769). *See* Edwards. M.
- Williams, David. S Jan TB Mar 1762 *Dolphin* but R for Army service same month. L.

Williams, David. SQS Bristol & TB to Md May 1763. G.

Williams, David. SQS Bristol Mar TB to Md Apr 1766. G.

Williams, David (1772). *See* Thomas. G.
Williams, Dorothy. S Bristol Sep 1737 AT Apr 1739. G.
• Williams, Edward. S Sep TB Dec 1758 *The Brothers* but R for sea service same month. M.
Williams, Elizabeth, spinster. S Bristol Sep 1734. G.
• Williams, George. S Lent R Jly T Sep 1764 *Justitia*. K.
Williams, George. S Bristol & TB to Md Apr 1767. G.
Williams, Henry of St. Ewen's. S Bristol May 1752. G.
Williams, James. S Bristol Jan 1742. G.
Williams, Jane. SQS Bristol May TB to Md Sep 1759. G.
Williams, Joan (1739). See Meredith. G.
Williams, John. S Lent R Jun 1727. Nt.
• Williams, John. S Summer 1739 R 14 yrs Feb 1740 TB to Va. De.
Williams, John. S Bristol Dec 1748. G.
Williams, John. SQS Bristol Aug 1767 TB to Md Sep 1768. G.
• Williams, John. S Bristol Aug 1770 R for life & TB to Va Mar 1771. G.
Williams, Judith, spinster. SQS Bristol Dec 1774 TB to Va May 1775. G.
Williams, Lydia. SQS Bristol Apr TB to Md Sep 1761. G.
Williams, Margaret. SQS Bristol Jun TB to Md Sep 1766 LC Annapolis from *Randolph* Mar 1767. G.
Williams, Martha, singlewoman. S Bristol Mar AT Sep 1740. G.
Williams, Mary. S Bristol Nov 1748. G.
• Williams, Mary. S s at St. Helen, Worcester, Summer but pardoned Oct 1761. Wo.
Williams, Mary. SQS Bristol Jun TB to Md Oct 1762. G.
• Williams, Mary. S Bristol Mar 1765 R 14 yrs & TB to Md Sep 1766 LC Annapolis from *Randolph* Mar 1767. G.
• Williams, Thomas. S Lent R Jly T Dec 1734 *Caesar*. K.
Williams, Thomas. R 14 yrs Bristol Mar 1741. G.
Williams, Thomas. SQS Bristol Sep 1764 TB to Md Apr 1765. G.
• Williams, Thomas *alias* Waters, Joseph. S Lent 1768. Bd.
• Williams *alias* Frost, William of St. Dunstan in East. R for America Aug 1715. M.
Williams, William. S Bristol Jan 1742. G.
Williams, William. S Bristol May TB to Md Aug 1769. G.
Williams, William *alias* Clivring, Peter. SQS Bristol & TB to Md Aug 1769. G.
• Williams, William. R Jly 1773 but allowed to T himself same month. M.
Williamson, George. S Bristol May AT Aug 1749. G.
• Williamson, John. SQS (Peterborough) s horse Aug R Sep 1718. No.
• Williamson, William. S Summer 1737 R Feb T 14 yrs Jun 1738 *Forward*. Sx.
Willis, John. SQS Bristol Dec 1769 TB to Md May 1770. G.

Willoughby, Elizabeth. S Bristol Aug 1748. G.
- Wills, Hugh. S Lent R 14 yrs Jun 1734. So.
- Wills, Samuel. S Lent but pardoned Apr 1760. No.
- Wilson, Ezekiel. R for life May 1765. De.

Wilson, James. S Summer 1743 R 14 yrs Feb 1744. E.

Wilson, James. S Lent R 14 yrs Jun 1764. K.

Wilson, Jane wife of Joseph of Hull, malt grinder. SQS Hull Epiphany TB Feb 1760. Y.

Wilson, John. R Jun 1714 & to remain in Newgate until transported. L.

Wilson, John. S Bristol May TB to Md Aug 1769. G.

Wilson, Joseph. R 14 yrs May 1739. La.

Wilson, Margaret, wife of John, soldier. S Bristol Jun 1734. G.

Wilson, Mary, aged 71, spoon caster. S Apr 1775 but in Morpeth Prison in Dec 1775. Nl.
- Wilson, Thomas. S Summer 1726 R Jun TB to Va Sep 1727. Le.
- Wiltshire, Isaac. S Lent R 14 yrs Jun TB to Va Sep 1744. Wi.

Winnall, Elizabeth. R 14 yrs Apr 1771. Wo.
- Winslett, John. S Aug 1765 R Feb T 14 yrs Apr 1766 *Ann*. Sx.
- Winslett, Samuel. S Aug 1765 R Feb T 14 yrs Apr 1766 *Ann*. Sx.

Winsley, William. S Lent R Jly 1728. Li.
- Wise, Edward. S Lent R 14 yrs Jun 1744 TB to Va 1745. De.
- Wiseley, Thomas. S Oct 1761 TB Apr 1762 *Dolphin* but R for Army service in Jamaica same month. M.

Witham, Arthur. S Lent R Jly 1730. E.

Withers, Thomas. S Bristol Jan AT Feb 1743. G.

Wood, Ann (1758). *See* Tindall. Y.
- Wood, James. R 14 yrs Lent 1768 [*not 1766*]. Nt.
- Wood, John. R Apr T 14 yrs Dec 1771 *Justitia*. Sy.

Wood, Mary. SQS Summer 1771. St.
- Wood, Obadiah. S for perjury Lent 1760 but R to serve in Army Jly 1761. St.
- Wood, Peter. S Summer 1757 R & T 14 yrs Apr 1758 *Lux* from London. Db.
- Wood, Susannah, spinster. S Bristol Apr 1767 R 14 yrs & TB to Md Sep 1768. G.
- Wood, Thomas. S Lent R 14 yrs Jun 1744 TB to Va 1745. De.
- Wood, William. S Mar R Jun T 14 yrs Sep 1758 *Tryal*. Sy.
- Woodbridge, Edward. S s sheep Lent R 14 yrs Summer 1765 but taken from ship in Downs & pardoned. O.

Woodhouse, Joseph of Leek Wootton. R for America Feb 1718. Wa.
- Woodhouse, Thomas. S Dec 1761 TB *Dolphin* but R for Army service same month. M.

Woodman, John. S Bristol Nov 1734. G.

Woodmansey, John of Sancton. SQS Beverley Easter 1775. Y.

Woods, Mary. SQS Bristol Oct 1764 TB to Md Apr 1765. G.

Woodward, John. S Bristol Feb 1750. G.
Woodward, John. S Bristol May AT Aug 1753. G.
Workman, Margaret, spinster. S Bristol Feb 1736. G.
• Worrall, Thomas. R Apr T Sep 1727 *Forward* LC Rappahannock May 1728. Sy.
Wricknorth, John. R for life Apr 1774. Sy.
• Wright, John. S Lent R Jly 1728. Li.
Wright, John. S 14 yrs Bristol Aug 1749. G.
• Wright, Joseph. S Lent R 14 yrs Summer 1760 but R for Army service Jly 1761. St.
Wright, Samuel. S Summer 1770. No.
Wright, Thomas. S Bristol Mar 1737. G.
• Wright, William. S Mar R Jun T 14 yrs Dec 1758 *The Brothers*. E.
Wynn, Mathew of St. Thomas's. S Bristol Sep 1752. G.

Yates, Geoffrey *alias* Henry of Warwick[shire]. R for America Feb 1696. Wa.
Yates, James. S Bristol Mar 1742. G.
• Yates, John. R 14 yrs Jun TB to Va Oct 1768. Wi.
• Yates, Willdy. S Lent R Jly T Sep 1730 *Smith*. Sy.
• Young, Ann. S Oct T Dec 1771 *Justitia* but taken from ship & pardoned same month. L.
Young, Honor. S Summer 1764. Li.
Young, John. R for life Jan 1772. L.
Young, Mary, spinster. S Bristol Feb 1753. G.
• Younger, Thomas. S Apr-Jun T Jly 1772 *Tayloe* but taken from ship & pardoned same month. M.

Zierny, Paul. R for life Apr 1751. K.

www.ingramcontent.com/pod-product-compliance
Ingram Content Group UK Ltd.
Pitfield, Milton Keynes, MK11 3LW, UK
UKHW020730190225
455309UK00010B/394